The Complete
RENAISSANCE
SWORDSMAN

A Guide to the Use of
All Manner of Weapons

ANTONIO MANCIOLINO'S *OPERA NOVA* (1531)

Translated and with a New Illustrated Introduction by
TOM LEONI

Freelance Academy Press, Inc.
www.FreelanceAcademyPress.com

Freelance Academy Press, Inc., Wheaton, IL 60189
www.freelanceacademypress.com

19 18 17 16 15 14 13 12 11 10   1 2 3 4 5

ISBN 978-0-9825911-3-0

Library of Congress Control Number: 2010931958

To My Father, Ezio Leoni

CONTENTS

FOREWORD . . . . *ix*

AUTHOR'S PREFACE . . . .*xiii*

ACKNOWLEDGEMENTS . . . .*xiv*

INTRODUCTION *1*

Martial Arts in Renaissance Italy *1*

Martial Arts and the Italian Renaissance:
What They Were, Who Taught Them, Who Learned Them *3*

Tackling Manciolino's *Opera Nova*:
A Primer of Bolognese Swordsmanship *16*

Lines, Measure, Tempo and Stances *25*

The Guards (*Guardie*) *28*

Footwork (*Passeggiare*) *37*

The Attacks (*Offese*): Moving Between the Guards *51*

Defense (*Difese*): Parries and the Role of the Buckler *53*

Other Actions and Definitions *56*

The Assalto and the Main Parts of the Play *60*

Attitude and Mental Disposition In Bolognese Swordsmanship *62*

Giovanni dalle Bande Nere, the Great Devil:
A Portrait of a Famous Swordsman of the Bolognese Style *64*

A Note on Language, the Translation, and on Editorial Decisions *69*

OPERA NOVA *71*

OPERA NOVA TO LEARN
How to Fight and Defend with any Sort of Arms,
Written by Antonio Manciolino, Bolognese *72*

HERE BEGIN A FEW
Main Rules or Explanations
on the Valiant Art of Arms *73*

**OF COMBAT AND FENCING WITH
ALL SORTS OF WEAPONS IN SIX BOOKS** 79

BOOK ONE 79

Chapter I: The Guards 79

Chapter II: The Blows 82

Chapter III: The Attacks from Guardia Alta 82

Chapter IV: The Counters to the Attacks from Guardia Alta 84

Chapter V: The Attacks from Guardia di Testa 84

Chapter VI: The Counters to the Attacks from Guardia di Testa 84

Chapter VII: The Attacks from Guardia di Faccia 85

Chapter VIII: The Counters to the Attacks from Guardia di Faccia . . . 85

Chapter IX: The Attacks from Guardia di Sopra il Braccio 85

*Chapter X: The Counters to the Attacks from Guardia di
Sopra il Braccio* 86

Chapter XI: The Attacks from Guardia di Sotto il Braccio 87

*Chapter XII: The Counters to the Attacks from Guardia di
Sotto il Braccio* 87

Chapter XIII: The Attacks from Porta di Ferro Stretta. 88

*Chapter XIV: The Counters to the Attacks from Porta di
Ferro Stretta* 88

Chapter XV: The Attacks from Porta di Ferro Larga 89

Chapter XVI: The Counters to Attacks from Porta di Ferro Larga . . . 89

Chapter XVII: The Attacks from Cinghiara Porta di Ferro 90

*Chapter XVIII: The Counters to the Attacks from Cinghiara
Porta di Ferro*. 91

*Chapter XIX: The Attacks from Coda Lunga e Alta
(Left Foot Forward)* 91

Chapter XX: The Counters to Attacks from Coda Lunga e Alta 92

*Chapter XXI: The Attacks from Coda Lunga e Stretta
(Right Foot Forward)* 93

*Chapter XXII: The Counters to the Attacks from Coda Lunga
e Stretta (Right Foot Forward).* 93

BOOK TWO 95

The First Assalto 95

The Second Assalto. 99

The Third Assalto 103

BOOK THREE 109

First Stretta, False Edge on False Edge. 110

Second Stretta, False Edge on False Edge. 110

Third Stretta, False Edge on False Edge 111

Fourth Stretta, False Edge on False Edge. 111

Fifth Stretta, False Edge on False Edge 111

Sixth Stretta, False Edge on False Edge 111

Seventh Stretta, False Edge on False Edge 111

Eighth Stretta, False Edge on False Edge 112

Ninth Stretta, False Edge on False Edge 112

Tenth Stretta, False Edge on False Edge 112

Eleventh Stretta, False Edge on False Edge 112

Twelfth Stretta, False Edge on False Edge 113

Thirteenth Stretta, False Edge on False Edge 113

Fourteenth Stretta, False Edge on False Edge 113

Fifteenth Stretta, False Edge on False Edge 113

Sixteenth Stretta, False Edge on False Edge 113

Seventeenth Stretta, False Edge on False Edge 114

First Stretta, True Edge on True Edge 114

Second Stretta, True Edge on True Edge 114

Third Stretta, True Edge on True Edge. 114

Fourth Stretta, True Edge on True Edge 115

Fifth Stretta, True Edge on True Edge 115

Sixth Stretta, True Edge on True Edge. 115

Seventh Stretta, True Edge on True Edge. 115

Eighth Stretta, True Edge on True Edge 115

Ninth Stretta, True Edge on True Edge 116

Tenth Stretta, True Edge on True Edge 116

Eleventh Stretta, True Edge on True Edge 116

Twelfth Stretta, True Edge on True Edge 116

Thirteenth Stretta, True Edge on True Edge. 116

Fourteenth Stretta, True Edge on True Edge 117

Fifteenth Stretta, True Edge on True Edge 117

Sixteenth Stretta, True Edge on True Edge 117

Seventeenth Stretta, True Edge on True Edge 117

BOOK FOUR 118

   Chapter I 119

   Chapter II 120

   Chapter III 121

   Chapter IV 121

   Chapter V 121

   Chapter VI 122

   Chapter VII 122

   Chapter VIII 122

   Chapter IX 124

   Chapter X 125

   Chapter XI: The Play of Two Swords 126

   Chapter XII: The Play of Single Sword 128

BOOK FIVE 130

   Chapter I: The Play of Sword and Cape 132

   Chapter II: Fencing Two Against Two With the Sword and Cape 135

   Chapter III: Fencing with the SPADA DA FILO *in the Right Hand and the Dagger in the Left* 135

   Chapter IV: Fencing with Sword and Rotella 136

BOOK SIX 140

   Play of Rotella and Partisan against the Same 141

   Another Play of the Same Weapons 142

   Play of Single Partisan 142

   Plays of Spiedo against Spiedo 143

   Plays of Ronca against Ronca 143

   Play of Hand-held Spears, One against One 144

FOREWORD

A BREEF REHERSALL OF THE CHIEFE CONDITIONS AND QUALITIES IN A COURTIER:

To be skilfull in all kynd of marciall feates both on horsbacke and a foote, and well practised in them: whiche is his cheef profession, though his understandinge be the lesse in all other thinges. To play well at fense upon all kinde of weapons.

– Castiglione, *The Book of the Courtier,*
English edition by Sir Thomas Hoby (1561)

Although Baldassare Castiglione's *Il Cortegiano* ("The Book of the Courtier") has been remembered as a treatise on the manners and courtly culture of the Renaissance gentleman, Castiglione himself explicitly reminded his audience that the courtier's profession was first and foremost that of arms, "though his understanding be the lesse in all other things." Whatever the reality of the knightly class's waning martial relevance at the turn of the 16th-century, swordsmanship was still seen as "the art that ennobles you," as wrote Castiglione's fellow Urbinese courtier, the master-at-arms Filippo Vadi.

Since Classical times, Western scholars have generally classified knowledge as either an *art* or *science*. Fencing, the study of armed conflict, has held an unusual role straddling the divide between the two, and been variously classified by its adherents as either art, science or both. As the creative application of a body of knowledge, swordsmanship was long seen as an art, indeed the foremost of the "Arts of Mars." But with the growing focus on scientific inquiry during the Renaissance, and the rationalist obsessions of the modern era, fencing masters increasingly sought to demonstrate that fencing was a science, based on geometrical theory and reducible to logical, repeatable patterns of "if-then" scenarios. Thus, over the centuries the "Art of Defense" became the "Art and Science of Defense" and finally the "Science of Defense."

Whatever the semantic debate over how to classify fencing, the truth is that it was a discipline born of necessity, and its adherents were pragmatists; thus the swordsmanship of the medieval knight was no less scientific than that of a baroque duelist, and the practice of a Napoleonic fencing master no less artistic than his Renaissance predecessors. What made a good swordsman was the ability to understand and internalize the theory of swordplay, to apply its principles to anticipate and control the opponent, and to act and react creatively while under pressure in the midst of combat. The fencing master required an additional skill: the ability to explain this theory to others and develop a clear, precise method for instilling its lessons and applications in *others*.

This brings us back to Castiglione. Mastery of the arts was the courtier's goal; to develop his skills at his chosen devotions to such a degree that masterful performance seemed casual, effortless, even disdainful; a quality Castiglione names *sprezzatura*. As Humanists, the mastery of rhetoric and grammar was seen to order the mind and display the courtier's acuity, education and cleverness, and therefore skill at letters was increasingly prized. However, if diversity was the courtier's *goal*, mastering the discipline of arms was his *duty*, even at the expense of the other arts and sciences; so it is only natural that not all swordsmen would wield their pens with the same dexterity that they did their swords. Certainly that is quite true of the famed Bolognese master-at-arms, Achille Marozzo, whose massive *Opera Nova* (1536) shows him to be a man never in want of a superfluous adjective, and whose first edition contains such profound statements as, "This is the first assault of the sword and buckler; it is called so, because it comes first."

It is thus ironic that Marozzo's work was repeatedly reprinted for over a century, and achieved much greater fame than another, earlier *Opera Nova*; a smaller, more concise, and far more elegant work, written by his contemporary and fellow Bolognese, Antonio Manciolino. We know nothing of Manciolino other than his book, originally written a bit more than a decade before Marozzo's. Yet its pages reveal an author who embodies Castiglione's ideal master of both arms and letters. In the preface to each of the six "books" which form his treatise, Manciolino speaks eloquently and passionately to the practice of swordsmanship as it was being taught and written about by his contemporaries. When he finds fault in their practice, as he often does, he applies his pen with the panache and fervor of the practiced essayist, such as the lambasting he delivers at the beginning of his book to masters-at-arms who emphasize collecting fees, rather than on producing talented students of arms:

> As it is a human virtue to be of service to others and to admit that nobody is self-generated, so I believe it is steely greed to place in a school what is there only for one's own benefit instead of that of others. Such are the principles of the aforementioned teachers, who do nothing but sell at a price the noble plays of our art, as if the Virtue of Arms had fallen into such a low state to spur some to brag about peddling her sacred limbs in schools. These men do not see that a blunt mind cannot be yoked alongside a sharp intellect; and that the Art is not a whore to be sold at a price.

Just to be sure that his audience appreciates both the timelessness of his subject, and the depth of his Humanist education, Manciolino can't help but call upon the Olympians to embellish his writing in his six introductions:

> Not grace, for just as rich fabrics adorn the charming and lovely Nymphs lightly treading on Mount Menalus or in the Lyceum, so does supple stepping embellish the blows of the dazzling sword. Were our weapon despoiled of its proper steps, it would fall into the darkness of a serene night being orphaned of the stars. And how can white-clad Victory be, where gentle grace is lacking?

The maestro works carefully to make it clear that he is an educated man, able to casually—dare we say, "disdainfully"—wield his knowledge of Aristotle, Cicero and the Epics to reveal the timeless truths conveyed in his book. But what makes Manciolino distinct from so many of his contemporaries is his ability to restrain himself; to know when he must put aside the hat of the scholar to write with the clarity of a man of action.

> *Noble reader, I consider it necessary at this juncture to explain my earlier declaration that I would leave this work bare of any literary ornament. If you examine the matter closely, you can but admit that there are many things which we deem praiseworthy in one situation while considering them utterly unfit for another.*
>
> *…he who fails to praise the splendid colors of polished literature, the elegance of well-composed speech and the harmony of poetry would be rightfully deemed insensible. Yet, it would be equally insensible to adopt the same form of speech in a topic for which it is unfit.*

Realizing, with a rather heavy heart, that his profession has condemned him to not write of ancient heroes or with a poet's vocabulary, but to constrain himself to speaking of thrusts, cuts, parries and practical matters related to their use, Manciolino promises the reader that:

> *With this, I wish to conclude that although I do not come before you as an orator, my speech will not be so rough as to be unworthy of comparison with that of other modern, more polished works—if not from its outside, at least underneath its surface.*

He is true to his word. In each of his six books, the maestro writes with a crisp, precise voice and succinctly lays out a rich curriculum for fighting with nearly the entire Renaissance arsenal. He does not claim that the guards, plays or solo forms that he details are of his own invention, quite the contrary, and we know from comparing the works of later Bolognese masters, particularly Marozzo, that Manciolino was part of a larger tradition of swordplay that was nearly a century old when he wrote, and it lived at least a century after his book saw print. His great achievement is in presenting the tradition in clear, often step-by-step, instructions that reveal not just his system's curriculum, but its pedagogy—its art and its science. By proceeding through the *Opera Nova*, step-by-step, sword in hand, the student learns the fundamental building blocks of the system (the guards and how to play from and against each), its artistic expression (the techniques of the *spada da gioco*), its most pragmatic applications (the techniques of the *spada da filo*), and a method to develop the *sprezzatura* that belies true mastery of the sword (the assalti, or solo forms). Each part has its place, and each is introduced at a very specific point in an unfolding system of instruction. For the modern reader, following the path Manciolino has laid out for his readers brings us on a journey not only into the grim art of the 16th-century *champ clos*, but into the mindset of the Renaissance man of action.

In this translation, Tom Leoni has sought to give a long underappreciated author his due by rendering his work in contemporary English, while preserving the careful changes of voice and style with which he originally wrote the different sections of his book. The poetic style of the introductions and the vehement dismissal of his competitors' practices juxtaposes with the concisely rendered technical and tactical instructions precisely as Manciolino intended in the original Italian. This was no small task, and reveals not only Tom's own gifts as a polymath, but no little literary *sprezzatura* of his own.

It is a pleasure to bring Manciolino's "little book" to an audience 500 years removed from when he wrote, truly making it a "New Work" once more.

GREGORY D. MELE
Wheaton, Illinois, May 25, 2010

AUTHOR'S PREFACE

I t is with much happiness and a deep sense of honor that I send this book to the printer. After nearly 500 years, (479, to be precise), Antonio Manciolino's *Opera Nova*, the first extant fencing work printed in the Italian language, sees the light again, this time in English.

I hope that making his work available to the larger historical and Western martial arts community will once and for all establish Manciolino as not merely an impersonal "earliest extant," but rightfully as the talented pedagogist who authored one of the most valuable, thorough and well-written Renaissance treatises on the Art of Arms.

I also hope that my short historical and technical introductions will sketch a meaningful context around his words, and make his instruction easier to follow by beginners and experienced students alike.

Lastly, I hope that a renewed understanding of Manciolino's treatise will lay to rest the misconceptions created around him by 19th-century fencing historians. While valuable, their work should itself be viewed in the context of history; their cultural biases should be a reminder that their conclusions are not definitive; and a more direct understanding of the original sources should gradually replace the second-hand repetition of some of their opinions.

But not wishing to treat Victorian and Edwardian fencing historians as I charge them to have treated Manciolino, I will now put my pen down and wish you good reading.

TOM LEONI
Alexandria, Virginia, May 2010.

ACKNOWLEDGMENTS

A big thanks to Ilkka Hartikainen for helping me with the revision. Also a great thanks to Greg Mele, Adam Velez and the editing team for contributing their expertise and professionalism to the quality (and timeliness!) of this publication.

INTRODUCTION

Martial Arts in Renaissance Italy

Michelangelo: *Your Holiness, how would you wish me to portray your statue's left hand? Would Your Holiness wish to be seen holding a book?*

Pope Julius II: *A book? Me? Do you take me to be a schoolboy? I want to be shown holding my sword.[1]*

When most of us think of Renaissance Italy, our minds immediately fill with the shapes and colors of art: the paintings of Leonardo, the statues of Michelangelo, the architecture of Palladio. We hear the lasting words of literature and philosophy: the epic poems of Ariosto and Tasso, the treatises and discourses of Machiavelli; and the echoes of exquisite music: the lute of Francesco da Milano, the motets of Palestrina. We recall the long shadows cast by the great families who shaped history: the Medici, the Borgia, the Gonzaga, the Sforza. Yet, when most Italian Renaissance men thought of themselves, their mind filled with martial dreams: let me be a man of arms, and let all other arts be but rich and necessary ornaments to my essence.

In Renaissance Italy, personal martial prowess was valued, studied and cultivated as the highest of gentlemanly virtues. With the possible exceptions of Classical Sparta and feudal Japan, few other cultures throughout history elevated this skill to such a noble rank. Sure, the Republican Roman citizen-soldier was expected to wield a sword in defense of his country, but this was a public duty, to be discontinued once the soldier returned home to his private life. Instead, the martial ideal of Renaissance Italy extended to both the private and the public realms. As a man of the sword, the ideal individual discussed in Castiglione's immortal *Book of the Courtier* is as skilled while serving his lord on the battlefield as he is in private matters of honor and in peacetime martial tournaments and displays.

To understand the reasons behind this glorification of martial ability, we need to look at the social and political landscape of Italy from the Middle Ages to the 1500s. After the fall of the Roman Empire, two powerful forces blended to form the values of a new society: on one hand, the Germanic invaders brought with them individualism, warrior spirit,

---

[1]   Galbiati, Castiglioni and Gessi, *Tu Es Petrus*, Damiani, Rome, 1950, p. 297. All translations are my own unless otherwise noted.

the cult of honor and the idealization of the woman; on the other, the indigenous culture tempered these new influences through the ideals of Christianity and the sophistication of Roman jurisprudence.[2]

Among the other effects it produced, this blend created the noble spirit of chivalry, which was to play such an important role in the cultivation and exaltation of martial arts and martial skills.

Politically, too, the situation in Italy was one in which the sword was often the arbiter of history-making events. The peninsula was a mosaic of city-states and small principalities. Some were ruled by powerful and ambitious families like the Medici in Florence, the Visconti and later Sforza in Milan, the Este in Ferrara and so on. Others, like Venice, were independent republics. But what most of these small states had in common was a feverish desire to expand their dominions through political or, most often, military means. For this reason, the history of Renaissance Italy is a history of constant warfare, ever-changing political alliances and never-ending conflict.

In this environment thrived the rather unique figure of the *condottiero*, a professional military leader who placed his armies at the service of families or cities, often achieving power, glory and fame that surpassed that of his employers. Names like Colleoni, Carmagnola, Sforza and Dal Verme are familiar friends to all who study this time period. In other cases, it was the powerful ruling families themselves who produced great men of war, such as the Montefeltro, the Malatesta and the Medici. In all cases, though, the profession of arms was associated with chivalry, nobility of action and with strength of character—at least ideally, if not always in practice.

In the mid-1500s, the Imperial power of Charles V put an end to many of Italy's internal struggles, and the figure of the condottiero quickly became obsolete. The individual initiative that had played such an important part in shaping all aspects of the Renaissance had succumbed to the vast Imperial apparatus of oneness and bureaucratic conformity. And Italy's position as a collection of warring yet politically powerful states was soon reduced to that of Garden of the Empire. Milan, the formerly ambitious city of the Visconti and Sforza, became impoverished under this new regime. Florence, the home of the Medici, Machiavelli and Michelangelo, lost its international luster. Even the Roman Catholic Church, under the stifling spirit of the Counter-Reformation, became ossified in a new orthodoxy.

But something did not die. The role of the arts as ennobling to the soul endured even through these times; and chief among the arts, martial skills remained one of the most essential and relevant aspects of a gentleman's essence.

---

[2] An interesting exploration of this topic in the context of Italian literature may be found in Mario Pazzaglia's *Letteratura Italiana: Testi e Critica con Lineamenti di Storia Letteraria*, Volume 1 (Zanichelli, Bologna, 1979).

Martial Arts and the Italian Renaissance: What They Were, Who Taught Them, Who Learned Them

We know from numerous textual references from the period that Renaissance swordsmen called their discipline a martial art: an *ars militaris* or military art. Even in modern circles, we are becoming accustomed to calling historical fencing a martial art. But what is a "martial art" and, most importantly, what was it in the 1500s and 1600s? How was it defined? Who taught it? Who learned it?

A martial art bears its name from two things: the adjective *martial* (or military) and the noun *art*. It is "martial" or "military" because it pertains to the domain of Mars, the ancient Roman god of war (Ares for the Greeks), and it is applicable to physical conflict, both public in the form of a conventional battle and private in the form of the duel or of acts of self-defense. In the Renaissance, there was not such a sharp distinction as we imagine today between battlefield and individual martial skills; both were seen as sides of the same coin, therefore bearing the same name of martial, or *military*, art. According to some sources, individual martial skills were seen as the nobler of the two, which is why most fencing and martial arts treatises of that time do not focus on how to survive a battle: if you mastered the art of fighting one on one, you had more than plenty individual skill for the battlefield. (More on this in the section about the duel.)

The word *art* had a much more specific and rational meaning then than it does now in commonsense English. An art was defined as a finite set of rules derived from reason and experience and designed to achieve a goal in a repeatable manner in any particular discipline. For instance, the rules of the art of grammar allow you to narrow down the infinite possibilities of word-combinations into a finite pattern designed to meet a goal in a repeatable manner, which is to communicate effectively. Likewise, the rules of the art of fencing allow you to narrow down the infinite possibilities of actions and positions into a finite pattern designed to meet a goal in a repeatable manner, which is to defend your person and inflict injury on the opponent.

One of the most important roles of art is that it allows you to learn discipline efficiently, saving yourself the trial and error process associated with learning by experience alone. And this is particularly valuable in an art designed to preserve your person: while, for instance, a trial-and-error approach in music would at worst cause you to produce a poor melody or harmony, death and dishonor could be the price paid in the art of arms. Just as importantly, art and its finite, orderly disposition of rules was seen as the perfect vehicle to impart instruction. So, art was not the whimsical and rule-free form of self-expression that we understand today, but rather the opposite.

In Renaissance Italy, fencing instructors were a diverse group of more or less private entrepreneurs. In his important fencing treatise, *Opera Nova*, Bolognese master Achille Marozzo lamented that instructors in his day no longer underwent public certification as they did "in the old days."[3] And since an organized, national fencing school (which brought

---

[3] Achille Marozzo, *Opera Nova* (1536), p. 47R: "Many start teaching without having the necessary knowledge; I think this is because there are no longer certified masters, as there were in the old days. Those could not have students before obtaining a license from other masters, while in our days anyone can call himself a teacher."

back certification) did not become the norm until the 1800s, a master's credentials in the Renaissance were oftentimes the fame of his teacher's name and the quality of the students he produced.[4]

We know from period accounts that a quick way to discredit an instructor or what he taught was to show that his students had lost their lives in duels or other personal skirmishes, while the greatest respect was shown to those whose students had a reputation for being a tough and hard-to-beat lot. Also, some cities with prestigious universities like Bologna and Padua were known to produce good fencing masters, whose reputations helped attract new university students from the four corners of Europe.

The question of who learned these arts is even more easily answered. Because of the prominent place that martial prowess occupied in the constellation of the ideal education, most gentlemen and noblemen flocked to fencing salles. Many of these would then go on to pursue military careers, using their martial skills on the battlefield. Notable examples of such men include count Guido Rangoni (1485–1539), a formidable condottiero who learned fencing under Guido Antonio di Luca, the same master as Achille Marozzo,[5] who dedicated his fencing treatise to him; and condottiero Giovanni de' Medici, also called Giovanni dalle Bande Nere (1498–1526), of whom we will speak later in the book.

Other men would enjoy their lives as members of Europe's patrician class, using their skills as dazzling displays of sporting prowess in friendly bouts before admiring audiences of peers; others yet would simply go on to live their everyday existence, using their skills to defend their lives and their honor when either came under threat. But all of them shared, at least idealistically, a place in that most gallant of brotherhoods, the brotherhood of the skilled at arms.

Fencing

Within the broad universe of martial arts or skills at arms, which included equitation, wrestling, jousting and shooting firearms, fencing emerged as the noblest activity. Fencing, or in Italian, *schermo*, meaning defense, screen or shield, was generally defined as the art of defending oneself with edged weapons, and could be exercised both with and without armor, on foot or on horseback. As earlier martial treatises show, fencing took many shapes.

---

[4] In the dedication to Count Guido Rangoni, Achille Marozzo speaks of his own famous teacher, "Maestro Guido Antonio di Luca, Bolognese, from whose school exited more warriors than did from the belly of the Trojan horse." In the posthumous edition of Marozzo's work (1568), famed painter Giulio Fontana dedicates the book to Giovanni Manriche, chamberlain to the Emperor, stating of Marozzo that "[he] was, the world knows, a most excellent Master of this noble art, [leaving behind] countless valorous students." Who some of these students were we learn on page 47R of the work, where Marozzo lists "Emilio Marscotto, Gioan Maria Gabiato, Battista Pellacano and several other military men of high rank" as being among his pupils.

[5] Achille Marozzo, op. cit., dedication to Count Guido Rangoni: "I was becoming certain [of your worth...] from the time you learned this discipline from the aforementioned Maestro Guido Antonio, taking [...] his teachings all the way to the stars through your military career." Rangoni is also mentioned by Viggiani as a fencer in this style (p. 73R).

In the first half of the 1500s, when Manciolino operated, it was the norm in Italy to fence with a single-handed sword in the right hand and a small, rounded buckler in the left; in other cases, a quadrangular shield or *targa*, a dagger, cloak, a dagger and cloak together, a large round shield called a *rotella* or even a second sword could all serve as the left-hand weapon.

By the mid-century, fencing had gradually come to be associated with the use of the sword alone, the defensive and offensive weapon *par excellence*. And although companion left-handed weapons never quite disappeared until the days of regulated sport-fencing, the norm to begin one's martial studies by mastering the single-handed sword on its own began in the mid-1500s. The most praiseworthy martial artist was he who would appear at a duel in nothing but his shirt-sleeves, and carrying nothing but his single-handed sword.

As the art of fencing became the art of using the single sword, weapon-makers began altering the configuration of their product to adapt to the new needs. By the mid-1550s, single-handed swords intended to be used without armor and without a companion weapon had developed a complex hilt designed to protect the fencer's hand, as well as to provide a mass in defense of the head and the forearm, which could previously be defended by means of a shield or with armor. The age of the rapier had begun.

The Four Types of Combat

Italian masters-at-arms expected that the fencing skills they taught would be put to the test in the salle, in impromptu self-defense, on the battlefield and in the dueling "field of honor." Although in each case they advocated adjustments in tactics, these adjustments occurred squarely within the same art. This is why—throughout the Middle Ages and Renaissance—speaking of a civilian sword-art as opposed to a military or a dueling art is anti-historical. For instance, fighting unarmored with sharp swords (*spade da filo*) called for the preference of low guards in an art that taught both high and low; fighting against multiple opponents in a battle situation called for the heightened use of the cut in an art that taught both the cut and the thrust; fencing a friendly bout before a highly-demanding audience of peers would call for elaborate flourishes in the salle that would obviously be left out in a duel or on the battlefield; and so on.

FENCING

The fencing salle, known as *scuola* or *teatro*, was where proficiency with the sword was acquired and maintained, and it was through friendly free-fencing bouts (called assalti to this day) that martial skills were refined against uncooperative opponents. Almost invariably, period masters recommend that students learning the art of the sword should first free-fence with (or at least under the strict supervision of) their instructor rather than with other students.[6] This was done to ensure that fencing could be learned in a structured way, bad habits could be identified and eliminated, and mistakes could be corrected right away under the master's expert eye.

---

[6] "Do not let any beginning student fence unless you are there—not for several days. The reason is that, if they make a mistake, you can correct them and make them understand how they should fence with any other but their master. Otherwise, they can acquire bad habits which would be hard to correct." Achille Marozzo, op. cit., p. 2V.

Fencing was learned with a practice-sword called the *spada da gioco* or (later) *smarra* or *fioretto*, of which several specimens still survive in museums and private collections.[7] As opposed to the real sword, the *spada bianca* or *spada da filo* (literally, "white sword" or "edged sword"), the practice weapon consisted of a normal hilt outfitted with a blade of quadrangular section, not unlike a much stouter version of a modern foil. The point resembles a large nailhead or even a musket-ball, which was often covered in leather. The weight and handling of this practice sword was up to the person using it and his instructor's advice: some period masters advocated practicing with a heavier sword to build strength and endurance, while others preferred the opposite to prolong practice without fatiguing the arm.[8]

As far as protective equipment, we do not have consistent indications of what precautions were taken to avoid pain or injury. Marcantonio Pagano, a Neapolitan master operating in the mid-1550s, speaks of a friendly match between two of his students using a variety of weapons; under their regular clothes, they wore armor, while "upon touching it, from their hats sprang a metal mask covering their face."[9] On the other end of the spectrum, Bolognese master Angelo Viggiani was among those who advocated practicing with sharp swords[10]—something that Manciolino explicitly warns against in Book Six; and Viggiani's description of a lesson involves no more protective equipment than regular clothes.

That injuries must have occurred is documented by several factors. For instance, Giuseppe Morsicato Pallavicini, a 17th-century Sicilian master, cited municipal laws specifically written to waive liability from students who involuntarily inflicted wounds on their fellow learners in the course of a fencing lesson. Those were undoubtedly different days, with a different understanding of personal liability.

SELF-DEFENSE

Although in Renaissance Italy policing in towns and rural areas was far stricter and more sophisticated than what we generally like to imagine in common lore, there was still a need for self-defense. The time in Western history when men carried swords as a matter of course is relatively short—roughly between the 1400s and the late 1700s. Several period masters describe actions and tricks suitable for self-defense situations. Here are some of them, although the list is by no means complete:

- Fiore de' Liberi (1409) teaches how to fend off an attacker while sitting down, using a short staff, a cape (i.e., a cloak) or even a rope.

- Pietro Monte (1509) instructs how to strike the opponent while drawing the sword from the scabbard.

---

[7]   I had the pleasure of examining one dated around 1550 in the Bargello museum in Florence.

[8]   For instance, Manciolino is among those advocating the use of heavier practice weapons (see Book One, in the Main Rules section); so does Alfieri in his 1640 work *La Scherma*, chapter 4. Among those advocating the opposite is Giacomo di Grassi, who in his 1570 work *Ragione di Adoprar Sicuramente l'Arme* states that students should begin with a very light weapon to get used to operating it with speed (p. 148).

[9]   Marcantonio Pagano, *Le Tre Giornate*, Naples, 1553, Day One (page number deest).

[10]   Angelo Viggiani, *Lo Schermo*, Venice, 1575 (posthumous), p. 52V: "With practice weapons, no man can acquire the necessary valor and courage, and learn the art perfectly."

- Ridolfo Capoferro (1610) illustrates in what attitude one must resort to the sword and draw it in what we would call today "a situation" (*un accidente*).

- Antonio Quintino (1614) teaches how to use the sword, the cape and a variety of improvised weapons against human and animal attackers, including dogs, snakes, buffalos, bears and bulls.

- Francesco Antonio Marcelli (1686) gives detailed instructions on how to fight with the sword and lantern at night.

Just like today, there were different laws in different towns specifying which weapons were legal to carry and which were not. The sword was one of the most universally accepted, which also accounts for its widespread popularity. However, we do know that in some towns and countries there were edicts that limited the maximum length of blade legally allowed, while in others shorter weapons such as the dagger were prohibited, "making all your sweat in learning its use quite futile," as fencing master Salvator Fabris laments in 1606.

At this point, though, we must make an important consideration specifically regarding self-defense in treatises dealing specifically with the sword. Most authors of such treatises emphasize instruction between two opponents armed with similar weapons. The reason is not a matter of speculation, because the masters themselves provide it: this is the only efficient way to learn the art of fencing, which can then be adapted to a variety of weapons and situations (including self-defense under more unpredictable conditions). In other words, learning in the controlled environment of the salle against an increasingly uncooperative opponent is the way to become a proficient swordsman who can then adapt his skills for a variety of situations—including safe free-fencing, dueling, self-defense and the battlefield.

THE BATTLEFIELD

The use of the sword on the battlefield in the age of Manciolino was quite different from what it was 200 years before. By the mid-1500s, the outcome of battles was increasingly decided by gunpowder and pike formations rather than by the sword. However, the sword still had an important role, as it was carried by the cavalry, by special units as well as by officers and even pikemen as a secondary weapon. Several Italian treatises from the 1600s illustrate the kind of sword used by infantry at the time, some even giving explicit directions about its length. For instance, Ferrarese master Bonaventura Pistofilo, who wrote a military treatise on pike, halberd and musket in 1621, specifies that the perfect sword at the side of a pikeman should have a blade not too much longer than three feet.[11]

Naturally, fencing masters speak of special tactics to be used in battle-like situations—for instance, specifying that it is profitable to learn to parry multiple blows with a single cut if confronted by several opponents at once.[12] But they also insist that the same principles of fencing apply, hence seeing no need to teach dueling and battlefield fencing as two distinct disciplines.

---

[11] Bonaventura Pistofilo, *Oplomachia*, Siena, 1621, p. 37.

[12] Salvator Fabris, *Lo Schermo Overo Scienza d'Arme*, 1606, p. 9.

THE DUEL

The *non plus ultra* of martial contexts in which a sword could be employed was dueling. As the noted dueling theoretician Giovanni Battista Pigna remarked in 1560, while in battle you could rely on your comrades for support and you could win or lose without ever unsheathing your weapon, in a duel one hundred percent of the opponent's attention would be devoted to one thing only: defeating you. There is no gradual entering of a duel, said Pigna, the way you can sometimes enter a battle: the moment the trumpet sounds, your opponent's single-minded purpose is that of attacking you and you only. So, to paraphrase Machiavelli, for you as the swordsman, the outcome of a battle relies partly on *virtue* and partly on *fortune*, the latter consisting of factors like your commanders' prudence, the nature of the terrain or the courage of your comrades; the outcome of a duel, on the other hand, is only the result of *virtue*. And for an institution originating from the concept of "Judgment of God," this should come as no surprise.[13]

An important aspect of the duel stems from what the duel was: a trial, a judgment, in which one of the two parties would prove the veracity of his cause weapon-in-hand. Weapons had to be perfectly matched. This means that if a sword of a certain length and a certain sharpness was the stipulated weapon, it was by that sword that you had to conquer your opponent. Producing a different sword (or, worse, a dagger) in such case would immediately reveal the falseness of your cause and the trial would be lost; in some situations, even resorting to kicks, punches or grapples in what should be a trial by the sword may invalidate or at least tarnish a victory, especially when these were random acts of brutality rather than recognizable close-combat techniques.

This concept of a clean victory, "beyond a reasonable doubt" as we would say in today's courtroom, was why some duelists such as Pietro Balletta[14] were praised, almost idolized, for reporting twenty successes without suffering as much as a scratch—and without ever resorting to tricks or profiting from lucky breaks such as the opponent dropping his weapon.

Lastly, in the duel, the *attore* or plaintiff had to deliver the first blow, and the defendant had to defend against it. This immediately invalidates the meme that certain Renaissance sword arts are inherently offensive, while others are inherently defensive: a swordsman of the time had to be equally versed in delivering the first blow and in waiting to defeat it.

It is in this environment that Antonio Manciolino operated and wrote his swordsmanship treatise. Let us now take a closer look at the style he described, as well as the fertile martial ground from which he (a Bolognese) came.

---

[13] Giovanni Battista Pigna, *Il Duello*, 1560, pp 95–96: "Fortuitous outcomes are directly proportional to fortune and inversely proportional to art. A fortuitous outcome is more likely in a battle than in a duel. There is therefore more art in the latter than in the former. The more the art, the more the excellence. Therefore, since it is more excellent to fight a duel one against one than to fight a battle (countless against countless), it takes more valor to graduate from a battle to the duel than the other way around."

[14] Pigna, op. cit., p. 161.

Bologna and the "Bolognese School"

Bologna, the city where Manciolino lived and operated, is the capital of the Emilia-Romagna region of Italy. This is the region that, geographically and culturally, marks the divide between peninsular, Mediterranean Italy and the middle-European regions of the North. Situated on the major Roman artery *Via Emilia*, Bologna has been a center of cultural fervor, innovation and learning since the early Middle Ages. The jewel in the city's crown was, and still is, the university (the *Studium*), which has attracted and produced world-class scholars since the year 1088.

Although archeological digs have revealed traces of a much older vintage, Bologna started its life around 650 BCE, as an Etruscan city by the name of Felsina, and was later renamed Bona by the Gauls when they conquered the city in the 2nd century BCE. After being a Roman province by the name of Bononia, it changed hands first to the Byzantines, then to the Lombards, the Germanic people that gave the neighboring region of Lombardy its name, and that perhaps further kindled the city's martial spirit.

During the Middle Ages, Bologna became an important *comune* (city state), and it remained one until 1507, when it became part of the Papal state. The most important family associated with the city was the Bentivoglio, which had a strong influence on Bologna's socio-political and artistic life between the 13th- and the early 16th-centuries.

Today, Bologna's university, palaces, medieval towers and historic center (much of it, unfortunately, destroyed during the Second World War) still speak to the visitor of the city's glorious past and cultured present. The musical dialect spoken by the locals, said by some to be heavy with ancient Celtic influence, along with the reputation for the friendliness of the Bolognese people, are second only to the world-famous Bolognese cuisine to make the city a favorite stop for tourists traveling the length of the peninsula.

Closer to our subject, among the arts developed in the cultural center of Bologna, fencing was to become one of the city's longest traditions. Thanks to the many primary Bolognese sources, as well as the works of 19th-century historians such as Gelli and Novati,[15] we have a sense of a genealogy of masters which proves how many important figures Bologna produced in the martial field:

- Nerio, active in Bologna as early as the 1300s.[16]

- Lippo Dardi, operating in the early- to mid-1400s. Besides a fencing master, he was a mathematician, astronomer and university professor.[17] His name is the reason why some today call this style the "Dardi school."

- Guido Antonio de Luca, active around the beginning of the 1500s, who was Achille Marozzo's instructor, and from whose school, as Marozzo states, "sprang more swordsman than from the belly of the Trojan horse."

---

[15] Unfortunately, 19th-century Italian authors were excellent at citing little-known facts, and terrible at noting their sources, making it extremely difficult to follow the "paper trail" back to their sources.

[16] Jacopo Gelli, *L'Arte dell'Armi in Italia*, 1906. Gelli does not give a reference to this fact.

[17] Marco Rubboli and Luca Cesari, *L'Arte della Spada* (Il Cerchio, Bologna, 2005) p. 9.

- Antonio Manciolino, who published the earliest extant Bolognese treatise some-time around 1522 or 1523, and whose second 1531 edition is the basis for this translation. As of this writing, Manciolino's work also has the distinction of being the earliest extant fencing treatise printed in the Italian language.

- Achille Marozzo, pupil of de Luca, who published his work, also titled *Opera Nova*, in 1536. While not as concisely written as Manciolino's book, Marozzo's treatise enjoyed much popularity at the time, accounting for several subsequent editions.

- Angelo Viggiani, whose treatise *Lo Schermo* was published posthumously in 1575.

- Giovanni dall'Agocchie, whose 1572 treatise *Dell'Arte della Scherma* deals mostly with the single sword.

- The Cavalcabo' dynasty, which spread beyond Italy and into France well into the 17th-century.[18]

- Alessandro Senese, who published his treatise in 1660.

- Paolo Bertelli, who published a proto-classical fencing treatise in 1800.

A recently-discovered manuscript (MS 345–346) from the Classense library of Ravenna has been commonly accepted to be in the Bolognese tradition, and is often referred to in the fencing community as the "Anonymous Bolognese." Linguistically, it contains many *lombardisms* (dialect-like variations of words or spelling common in the North of Italy); stylistically, it is consistent with the teachings of Manciolino, Marozzo, Viggiani and dall'Agocchie. However, there is no direct evidence that its author hailed from Bologna. Another unknown is its date: some like Rubboli and Cesari see it as an early-1500s work, while I agree with others who place it about fifty years later. Regardless, it is one of the most important works in the Italian tradition, not only because of its length, but also because of the thoroughness with which it deals with certain weapons—especially the single sword.

So, can we speak of a "Bolognese style"? As far as I am aware from having examined the works I have listed above, none of the masters of the time did so. It is true that the works of the Bolognese masters (at least until and including dall'Agocchie) are much more consistent with each other in terminology, pedagogy and style than with those coming from other parts of Italy. Also, while never calling their style "Bolognese," masters from that town always include their provenance with their names, suggesting at least civic pride and at most a sense of belonging to a great martial tradition associated with the city itself.

On the other hand, some masters, such as Viggiani[19] and Pagano[20] hint at there being a common style in the era. The similarity of many actions and guards (along with some of their names) found in treatises from Germany to Southern Italy is corroborating evidence to this theory. It is therefore possible that what we call today the "Bolognese style" is nothing

---

[18] Rubboli and Cesari, op. cit., p. 11.

[19] Angelo Viggiani, op. cit., p. 81V: "This is the common defense—the one that every master will teach you."

[20] Marcantonio Pagano, op. cit., Third Day, page number deest: "I will therefore say that common play consists of learning the *gioco largo* [wide play], then the *gioco stretto* [narrow play]."

but a pedagogical tradition teaching a subset of what was that era's common style. I tend to believe this theory more than I do speculations of master-student relationships between otherwise unrelated authors. But wanting to remain intellectually honest, I can only state that this, too, is a theory and nothing more, since the evidence is inconclusive either way.

What We Know about Manciolino: the *Opera Nova* and Its Likely Dating

As important as Manciolino is for both the quality of his treatise and the fact that his is the first extant fencing text in printed Italian, we know little or nothing of him. Most of what we know, we can infer or speculate from reading his treatise.

Antonio Manciolino must have been born sometime in the second half of the 1400s. As of this writing, the only extant edition of his work *Opera Nova* is a subsequent one (likely the second), and it bears the date 1531. It is not known whether the master had contributed to the editing of the second edition, or indeed whether he was still alive to see it published. We know it is not the first edition for two reasons: it bears the words "newly revised and printed" and it is dedicated to a man who was dead by 1531.

So, how can we date the first edition more precisely? The vital clue is in the dedication, which is to Luis de Cordoba, ambassador of the Emperor to Adrian VI. Adrian's papacy is a short one—between his election in January 1522 and his death in September 1523—thus already narrowing down the probable date of first publication. But further clues enable us to pinpoint the date even more precisely.

A letter dated Oct. 8 from the soon-to-be former ambassador to the pope, Don Juan Manuel, informs the Emperor that, finding it abominable to serve a pope such as Adrian VI, he has asked Don Luis Fernandez de Cordoba, Duke of Sessa, to serve in his stead. Don Luis has his first conversation with the pope on or around Oct. 17, in the presence of his predecessor. By November, however, the pope already expresses irritation with his new ambassador, who privately tells Charles V "I'd rather fight a hundred campaigns in one day than have a single audience with the pope."[21]

Although from the spring of 1523 until the pope's death on Sept. 14, 1523, Don Luis is often absent to tend to his ill wife (who will die in 1524 and leave him a heartbroken widower), he does not formally relinquish his post. It is in October 1523 that Luis receives the honors of membership in the Order of the Golden Fleece by Charles V. This fact would have likely been mentioned by Manciolino in a fawning dedication, so the *Opera Nova* probably predates this honor.

In any case, with the election of Pope Clement VII on Nov. 19, 1523, Luis is de facto no longer "ambassador to Adrian VI." Manciolino's first edition is therefore likely to date somewhere between October 1522 and October 1523.

---

[21] Information in this paragraph is from correspondence cited *in toto* in Gustav Adolf Bergenroth's, *Calendar of State Papers, Spain, Vol. 2, 1509–1525* (1866).

Manciolino does not say who his teacher was. It may be possible that, like Marozzo, he had studied with de Luca, since the terminology, the actions and the pedagogical presentation are remarkably similar between these two authors. Still, we cannot be certain as of today.

Curiously, his work is not referenced in 17th-century fencing treatises that list past masters and their work. For instance, both Pallavicini (1670) and Marcelli (1686) name other Bolognese masters such as Marozzo, Viggiani and dall'Agocchie, but make no reference to Manciolino. The reason for this can only be the object of speculation. Was Manciolino's work simply no longer known a century and a half later? Was the circulation of his book not sufficiently large? If so, what warranted printing a second (or subsequent) edition in 1531? Again, we just don't know.

Much more egregiously, Manciolino's writings have been mischaracterized and misunderstood by fencing historians from the Victorian era. British historian Egerton Castle, for instance, dismisses Manciolino's work as being long on dueling jurisprudence, short on fencing, and of containing four guards, only one of which is useful.[22] A mere skimming of the work of the Bolognese master proves this to be false: Manciolino talks about fencing in all but the short introductions to each of the six books, in the fifth one of which he unmistakably makes a point as to why he *will not* include any dissertations on dueling law. Manciolino also counts and names ten main guards, while using a handful more.

Italian historian Jacopo Gelli[23] uses this blunder to pounce on his rival Castle, understandably accusing him of not having even cracked the *Opera Nova* open. But, himself not to be outdone, Gelli damns Manciolino's chapter on polearms as setting back the art's evolutionary clock; and he states that Manciolino, a mere man of the sword, could not possibly have penned the linguistically refined introductions to the preface and his six books.

Indeed, Manciolino's work is exquisitely written, and the author reveals himself to be not only an expert pedagogist, but also a man of refined sensibility. One of the reasons that spurred me to translate this book is the hope that the master's work may shine of its own light to an international audience, thus rectifying the stubborn, even willful, misunderstandings of 19th-century historians; these misunderstandings live on as "authoritative" whenever quoted by those who do not have the means to read the *Opera Nova* in the original Italian. After more than a century of being misunderstood and misused, Manciolino deserves his day.

The Structure of the *Opera Nova*

The *Opera Nova* (Italian for "New Work") is what seems to be a small octavo, measuring approximately nine inches by five. It is 63 pages long, each page being recto/verso—thus making it (in modern terms) 126 pages long—and it is printed in an elegant italic font quite

---

[22] Egerton Castle, *Schools and Masters of Fencing*, 1858: "Manciolino's text is so much filled up with wise dissertations on the rules of honour and way of picking and deciding quarrels in a gentlemanly manner, that very little actual 'fencing' has found its way into his little work. Of the four guards therein described, the only one recognizable as being intended for any definite purpose, is a 'high guard' somewhat similar to the modern head parry."

[23] Jacopo Gelli, op. cit.

common in 16th-century Italy. It contains a dedication, an introduction listing some rules and general advice to the swordsman, and six books each dealing with a distinct concept, weapon-combination or group of weapons:

1. The main guards of sword and buckler, as well as the attacks and counters that can be performed from each.

2. Three assalti with the sword and buckler.

3. The *strette* of the half-sword, with the sword and buckler.

4. The play of sword and large buckler or square targa; the play of two swords; the play of single sword. This whole book deals with the *spada da filo*, or sword with sharp edges as opposed to a practice sword.

5. The *spada da filo* and cape (or cloak) taught in single combat and with two fencers against two; *spada da filo* and dagger; *spada da filo* and *rotella* (a large round shield).

6. Polearms: partisan and rotella, partisan alone, *spiedo*, *ronca* (bill), and spear.

From a pedagogical standpoint, the book contains only text. The eight small woodcuts (one in the frontispiece, one at the beginning of the introduction, and one at the opening of each book) are for ornament only, and, although depicting martial scenes, they are not strictly related with the content of the chapters in which they are placed.

The introduction and the six books are each preceded by a short and elegantly-written dissertation on Manciolino's teaching and writing philosophy. These sections reveal an author who was deeply passionate about teaching, who cared about good writing, who greatly enjoyed the Classics (particularly Aristotle and Greco-Roman mythology) and who knew how to ridicule and refute his critics. In all, they add much color to this pedagogical work, and they give us a glimpse into the heart and mind of the man who penned it.

The Pedagogy of the *Opera Nova*

A brief pedagogical excursion through Italian martial literature in the pre-classical era, that is, between the early-1400s and the 1600s, place Manciolino's style quite in the middle—not only chronologically, but formally and stylistically.

The earliest Italian martial works of which we have evidence are those of Fiore de' Liberi (1409) and Filippo Vadi (approximately mid-1480s); these are structured mostly in verse, the goal being to encourage the student to memorize as much as possible of the text and therefore the art.[24] Among the many things these two texts have in common is the fact that plays are illustrated and accompanied by a short description in verse. In Vadi's text, however, there is also a long, text-only introduction that explains the main tenets of the art. This section is possibly the precursor to the next century's main pedagogical structure, which is predominantly text only.

---

[24] For instance, Fiore de' Liberi states: "Galeazzo used to say that without books, nobody can truly be a master or student in this art. I, Fiore, agree with this: there is so much to this art that even the man with the keenest memory in the world will be unable to learn more than a fourth of it without books." Fiore de' Liberi's *Fior di Battaglia* (1409), p. 3V.

With very few exceptions (such as Agrippa and Lovino),[25] the main body of fencing pedagogy in Italy is delivered by text—which is absolutely the case with Manciolino. Marozzo and Viggiani have a few plates illustrating the guards, but none of the actions are represented visually the way they were a century before. The two vestiges of the previous century's pedagogical structure found in Marozzo are the presence of a *segno*, which is the illustration of the direction of the cuts, and the fact that he depicts his dagger and wrestling plays in Book Six—but these, too, are the exceptions in a century in which the text was to be relied upon, almost solely, to memorize and look up fencing actions.

Illustrated actions reappear in the first half of the next century, where the prevalent mode of written fencing pedagogy seems to gravitate towards a text-only introduction of the main terms of the art, followed by an illustrated explanation of the main actions. This is the model followed by rapier masters Salvator Fabris and his contemporaries.

The question is, how was a book such as Manciolino's supposed to be used? The answer can be found in the words of some contemporary masters.

In his 1509 work *Artis Militaris Collectanea*, Pietro Monte states:

> *I have often meditated about how feeble and fragile man's memory is; and how quickly what we learn and say is allowed to fade away. I decided to write this compendium so that part of the things and the exercise that we have used among us for some time may be more easily remembered. This discourse will easily and briefly present a whole series of terms, although it is not the intent to explain all parts in great detail. If you are familiar with this discipline, it is sufficient to remember some of the paths of the whole journey, and from there the road easily broadens and spans the whole subject.[26]*

Marozzo echoes this purpose, stating:

> *In this book, I will write many, many things about the art of fencing, so that you can memorize all that you have learned from me. I am doing this so that you can recollect things even if you have not practiced for a long time. Be advised that few can truly understand what is in this book; the exception is you, who have studied with me with such assiduity. Let me also advise you that you should read this book a few times, then practice sword-in-hand, so that with a little toil the play can come back to your mind.[27]*

It is rather clear, then, what the function of a fencing text was. Its primary pedagogical role was to help students already familiar with swordsmanship memorize the art; its secondary role was to aid students who may have forgotten some actions remember them after looking them up and practicing them sword-in-hand.

---

[25] Camillo Agrippa, *Trattato di Scientia d'Arme*, Rome, 1553; and Antonio Lovino, *Traite' d'Escrime* (circa 1580).

[26] Pietro Monte, *Artis Militaris Collectanea*, 1509, prologue.

[27] Achille Marozzo, op. cit., p. IV.

Little did these men know that these arts would be allowed to die, and that five hundred years later they would be rediscovered and pieced together (as much as possible) using their printed words. Had they known this, I am sure their explanations would be much more thorough, their definitions more exact and their illustrations more abundant. Still, by comparing and contrasting the extant fencing treatises of the time, we can cobble together at least some of the lost knowledge that each writer assumed of his readership. This is all the more the case with what we call "Bolognese swordsmanship," since there is a great deal of consistency in the guards, the attacks, the parries, the steps and the structure of the play in general. In other words, a careful study of all extant contemporary texts can hopefully place us closer to the "few" who can "understand what is in this book," in the taunting words of Achille Marozzo.

Tackling Manciolino's *Opera Nova*: A Primer of Bolognese Swordsmanship

T he actions, steps, attacks, defenses and other techniques presented by Manciolino are the perfect representation of the style we call "Bolognese." Many of the same concepts are also found in swordsmanship treatises from the 1400s to the 1600s, particularly in those of Marozzo, Viggiani, dall'Agocchie and the so-called "Anonymous Bolognese." As such, most of the contents of his text will be familiar to those who study the style.

However, since his text contains no detailed explanations of the fundamentals, it would be of value to add a basic primer for swordsmanship students of all levels, so that they may better understand Manciolino's instruction. This primer contains most of the terminology, concepts and actions found in his *Opera Nova* and other Bolognese texts, explained in simple terms to help you *recognize* and *visualize* the actions, concepts, definitions and positions described by Manciolino.

Note: whenever possible, you will find the original terminology literally translated and with the original Italian in parenthesis. When the original terminology is not present—the masters giving instead a long description for an action or concept—I have used new terms, giving Manciolino's original wording in the description.

The Sword (*Spada*)

Which sword should be used for Manciolino's swordsmanship style? As with most historical fencing styles, Manciolino's was not intended to be a user's manual of sorts for a particular sword-type; rather, it was a universal set of instructions aimed at knowing how to use most swords—or indeed most edged weapons. In Chapter 25, Achille Marozzo tells us that a great number of actions and principles apply to a gamut of weapons and weapon-combinations going from the single dagger to the sword (used with or without companion weapons held in the other hand), and even to the *spadone* or two-handed sword.

Italian sword with a simple hilt, c. 1500 – Museo Nazionale di Capodimonte

Also, in an era when judicial dueling was in its apogee, the choice of swords was the right of the defendant; therefore, the plaintiff had to quickly adapt his skills to his adversary's choice, thereby rendering absurd the proposition that any 16th-century fencing style could only work with a particular type of sword. Since it is amply documented that this style was used in both military and civilian situations, it follows that both military and civilian swords would have been used. Thus, any non-specialized sword used in the 16th-century would be a good fit to learn this style. In the introductory section, Manciolino also mentions that different blade-lengths may be used, saying that practicing with shorter swords is a good way to learn parrying.

Hilt-types illustrated by Marozzo and Viggiani range from a simple cross to a rapier-like "swept-hilt," such as A.V.B. Norman's type 74 (aptly dated from around 1560). Viggiani (54R) mentions the additional hand protection added to hilts in recent years, which matches what we know about the evolution of the sword in the 16th-century.

As far as the blade, 16th-century originals show a dizzying variety of configurations, from the wide to the narrow, from the long to the short, from the pronouncedly tapered to the straight-sided. Although he does not favor them, Viggiani also mentions the use of straight, single-edged blades or "backswords."

My recommendation is to use a practice sword that is not much heavier than two-and-a-half pounds, so that the style's many flourishes may be performed at the appropriate speed without unduly fatiguing the arm. The period practice swords I have examined were consistently on the lighter side, being mostly within two pounds.

Sword of Ettore Fieramosca, dated 1513 – Museo Nazionale di Capodimonte

Blade length should be proportionate to the person using the sword, with feet-to-navel length being the absolute upper limit (measured from the crossguard). For most people this will produce a sword with a blade between thirty-two and forty inches in length.

Hilt types are the choice of the student. If the many cuts to the swordsman's hand are to be practiced with any sort of vigor, I recommend a hilt that protects the hand, such as A.V.B. Norman's type 51 or something similar. An important consideration: the illustrations in Marozzo clearly show that placing the index finger beyond the cross-guard and around the ricasso was a common way to hold the sword; therefore, I recommend a hilt that enables the student to do so.

An important part of the choice of swords is the point of balance: this should be approximately four inches from the crossguard. A blade-heavy sword will fatigue the arm, while a pommel-heavy one will cause many thrusts to miss high, while reducing the effectiveness of the cut. Choose a well-balanced blade that has a well-developed point and enough presence to cut well, and you will not go wrong.

The sword-blade has two edges and a point; it also has a forte (strong) and a debole (weak).

True edge (*filo dritto*) – The edge of the sword pointing towards the ground when the sword is carried in the scabbard.

False edge (*filo falso*) – The edge of the sword pointing up when the sword is carried in the scabbard.

Point (*punta*) – The sharp extremity of the blade. Its role is to penetrate the target in the course of thrusting actions.

Forte (*forte*) – The half of the blade closest to the hilt; its role is primarily defensive.

Debole (*debole*) – The half of the blade containing the point; its role in this style is both offensive and defensive. The offensive role consists of delivering thrusts and cuts. The defensive role consists in the stylistically-typical *falso* parry, in which the debole of the false edge is employed in beating away the incoming attack with a cut.

Note: we know from dall'Agocchie (p. 21R) that most true-edge parries are performed with the forte, while most false-edge parries are executed with the debole.

Holding the Sword

None of the early-16th-century masters describe how to hold the sword. However, as I have mentioned above, period illustrations from contemporary swordsmanship treatises show that, most of the time, the sword is held with the index finger looped over the crossguard and around the ricasso. The middle, ring and little fingers should be wrapped solidly but not too tightly around the handle, while the thumb may rest on the tip of the index finger, on the quillon-block or even on the back of the blade. If you feel your hand cramping as you train with the sword, or the quillons bite into the webbing between your thumb and index finger, you are holding the sword too tightly.

This way of holding the sword makes thrusting natural and accurate, while in no way hindering the delivery of powerful cuts.

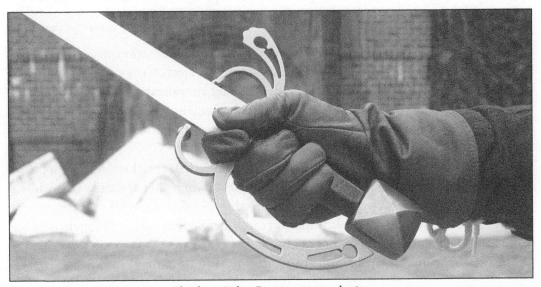

The classic Italian Renaissance sword-grip.

The Buckler (*Brocchiero*)

The buckler, also called the "small buckler" (*brocchiero stretto*) is the main defensive weapon held by the hand not wielding the sword. Iconography and surviving museum specimens indicate that this is a rounded shield, approximately ten inches in diameter. Unlike the targa, which could be made of different materials including wood, leather and even parchment, the buckler was almost invariably made of iron. The main parts of the buckler are as follows:

The edge or rim (*orlo*) – This is the outer circumference of the buckler, and it is almost always reinforced by a plain or roped band of metal to better withstand the opponent's blows.

The face (*penna*) – If we look at the buckler as a series of concentric circles, this is the portion contained between the rim (the outer circle) and the boss (the inner circle). The face of the buckler may be concave or convex in shape, and it may or may not contain ribbed radii. There is an inner face and an outer face: the former is the side facing you as you hold the buckler, while the latter is that facing the opponent.

The boss (*coppola*) – This is the dome-shaped inner circle of the buckler, which is always convex if seen from the opponent's viewpoint; its role is to contain the wielder's hand on one side, and to be able to deliver strikes to the opponent's face on the other.

The handle (*manico*) – This is a C-shaped bar more or less cylindrical in section, with either end riveted to the inner face of the buckler so as to bridge the concavity of the boss. Its function is to provide a secure grip for the buckler. It should therefore be substantial enough to fill the hand without being unwieldy.

HOLDING THE BUCKLER

Proper instruction on how to hold the buckler is lacking in Bolognese literature, but the way it is commonly taught today is to wrap the left hand's index, middle, ring and little fingers around the handle while holding the thumb flat against it. In the on-guard position, the hand is held with the palm facing right, so that the face of the buckler is perpendicular to the ground and points squarely at the opponent.

A Few Definitions Concerning the Other Weapons

We have already seen the two main weapons used in this style, the sword and the small buckler. Let's now take a quick look at the other weapons mentioned and used by Manciolino, starting with the other types of shield, touching upon the dagger and the cape, and spending a few words on the polearms used in the period.

The wide buckler (*brocchiero largo*) – This is essentially a slightly larger version of the small buckler that Manciolino and Marozzo use in the assalti. Practically, I recommend using a round buckler with a diameter between twelve and fourteen inches. Note: all the illustrations in Marozzo showing a round buckler are meant to represent the wide buckler, as he states in chapter 137 of his Book II, where he also specifies that the nature of the guards is similar regardless of the companion weapon held.

The targa (*targa*) – This shield is considered to be quintessentially Italian. It is shaped like a square, rectangle or trapezoid, and its face is not flat, but features a recurved surface with a central convexity and flaring sides. Its size should roughly match that of the wide buckler, since in Manciolino the plays of one are interchangeable with those of the other. This shield could be made of metal as well as of softer materials such as leather or parchment, in which case it could be jammed against the opponent's point to temporarily trap his blade, as the Anonymous Bolognese details on page 18V of Volume II in his treatise. The targa is gripped the same way as the small buckler; however, the on-guard position features the shield held obliquely with its top-left corner facing up and forward (see first picture on p. 36). The targa is also one of the longest-lived shields in Italian martial literature, appearing as late as 1696 in conjunction with the rapier, in the treatise *La Spada Maestra* of Venetian master Bondi' di Mazo.

The rotella (*rotella*) – This is the largest of the shields used by Manciolino. It is a round shield of a diameter of eighteen to twenty inches or larger, with a slightly convex face. Museum originals may appear as smooth, radially ribbed or fluted, and they may or may not contain a short central spike called a *brocco*. The rotella's large surface presented a perfect canvas for the engraver, which is why it is common to encounter surviving examples of elaborately engraved or chiseled rotelle.[28] The rotella was also used in conjunction with other weapons such as the partisan and the spear, and was employed both on foot and on horseback. It is held by sliding the left arm through a strap, then grasping the handle or a second strap with the left hand.

The shields in Manciolino's system and their comparative size. Top: targa (left) and small buckler (right). Bottom: rotella (left) and wide buckler (right).

---

[28] Modenese master Giacomo di Grassi states on p. 76 of his 1570 treatise: "...this weapon is so honored and prized that, besides employing it [as a weapon...], princes, lords and gentlemen use it to richly ornate their homes."

The dagger (*pugnale*) – Marozzo illustrates the dagger in different guises. When he depicts it in conjunction with the sword, the dagger appears as small weapon, not dissimilar from the left-handed dagger used by later generations in conjunction with the rapier; when used alone or with a cape, it becomes a larger dagger that could qualify as a short sword. In one instance, Marozzo also calls the dagger *Pugnale Bolognese*, which creates a number of interesting questions. Which daggers were typically Bolognese? Does Marozzo intend to differentiate it from other daggers? The illustration corresponding to the qualifier *Bolognese* shows a short-bladed weapon with small, straight quillons, held with the thumb flat on the quillon-block. In subsequent chapters, Marozzo illustrates a substantially larger dagger, in one instance gripped like a sword with the index over the quillons. The only dagger typical of the Emilia-Romagna region (of which Bologna is the capital) is the weapon commonly known as *cinquadea* or *cinquedea*, which is a wide-bladed, pronouncedly-tapered dagger with one or more fullers along its length. Here is when we must remember that a martial art is not one that is a mere "user's manual" for a specific kind of weapon, but may be adapted to different variations within a weapon family.

Swords and daggers suitable for the Bolognese style. From left to right: cross-hilted Venetian sword, parrying dagger, Milanese rapier, cinquadea dagger, Venetian infantry sword.

The cape (*cappa*) – This was a common article of clothing worn throughout the Renaissance; it typically consisted of a short, sleeveless woolen overcoat with a collar, worn over the left shoulder and held in place by a tie or ribbon that passed under the opposite arm. It was a very common defensive weapon between the 15th- and the 18th-centuries, since it was widely available and never subjected to legal restrictions, as often happened with the dagger and other left-handed arms. As a weapon, the cape was held by grabbing one end with the fingers of the left hand, then turning the left arm counterclockwise so as to cause the cape to wrap itself one or more times around the forearm up to the elbow. The excess fabric should hang to the outside of the left arm (i.e., to the left), and be neither too long nor too short, so as to balance the need for mobility without fear of tripping and of defending the lower body.

The partisan (*partigiana*) – The partisan was a polearm commonly used in Italy between the late 1400s and the early 1600s. It consisted of a broad-bladed, sharply tapering, double-edged iron mounted on a haft. It also had a pair of short protrusions jutting out of the base of the blade, which became more prominent and more elaborate in the course of the 17th-century.

Guard of partisan used without shield.

Guard of partisan and rotella, with both hands holding the weapon.

Guard of partisan and rotella, with single-handed, overhand grip.

The spiedo (*spiedo*) – The spiedo was another type of polearm used predominantly in the 16th-century. Its iron consisted of a central, narrow, two-edged blade sided by two additional wing-shaped blades capable of both inflicting injury to the opponent and trapping his weapon with a technique known as *inforcatura*.

The ronca (*ronca*) – Also called the "Italian bill," the ronca was considered a formidable weapon, since it could inflict injury in all directions, that is, not only by going forward or sideways, but also by being withdrawn. Originating from a common medieval pruning tool, it has an asymmetrical iron consisting of the following elements. On one side, there is a true edge shaped like a convex axe and topped by the horn or *corno*, a crescent-shaped blade sweeping back towards the butt of the weapon. On the other side, there is a stout spike. On top, there is a double-edged or quadrangular thrusting blade, while at the bottom of the iron there are normally two short lugs. The ronca became superseded by the halberd which, like the ronca, could also inflict injury in any direction.

Note: Florentine 16th-century master Francesco Altoni states that the spiedo and the partisan are roughly the same size. Pietro Monte, author of the 1509 treatise *Artis Militaris Collectanea*, states that the partisan should be as high as a man holding his arm vertically above his head, and that the ronca is of a similar size. For all intents and purposes, these three weapons should be regarded as comparable in size (approximately eight feet in total length).

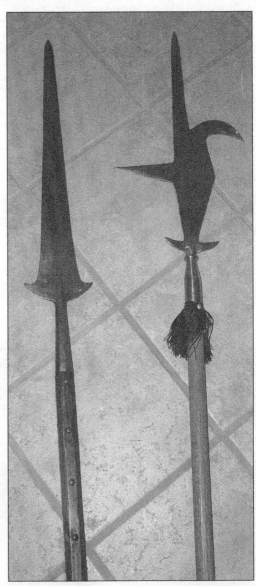

Two typically Italian polearms used by Manciolino: the partisan (left) and the ronca (right).

The spear (*lancia*) – This is a polearm consisting of a long haft (roughly two or three arms' lengths longer than the partisan, spiedo and ronca) and a small, leaf-shaped blade that, although possessing two edges, makes the weapon almost exclusively a thrusting one.

Note: polearms were often outfitted with an iron spike or cap at the end of the butt, so that either end could be used offensively.

Lines, Measure, Tempo and Stances

Before we start delving into the mechanics of the style, here are some definitions that will greatly clarify what follows. Whenever possible, I will offer a reference as to where these definitions may be found in the context of early-16th-century Italian swordsmanship.

Note: All actions described in this section assume right-handed fencers.

The line – Called *strada* by 15th-century master Fiore de' Liberi, *dritta via* by the "Anonymous Bolognese" (p. 24V) and *retta linea* in the next century, this is generally two things: a) the imaginary line on the ground representing the shortest distance between two opposing fencers (called the "line of direction" in classical fencing) and b) the line of offense, i.e., the imaginary line going from one fencer's chest to the other's.

On-line and off-line – These two terms refer to the degree of divergence from the line in the context of a position or action. "On-line" means on or parallel to the line. "Off-line" means away from or diverging from the line. There is no consistent period terminology for these concepts.

Inside and outside (*dentro* or *dentrovia* and *fuori* or *fuorivia*) – Most often, these two terms mean the following: you are inside when the opponent's blade is to the left of yours. You are outside when the opponent's blade is to the right of yours.

Measure (*misura*) – Measure is defined by Viggiani (p. 61R) as the distance between you and the opponent from which you can strike him with an *accrescimento* (see below for definition) or a pass. In other words, it is the distance between you and the opponent from which you can strike him with no more than a single step.

Tempo (*tempo*) – Tempo, Italian for "time," means three things in this style of fencing.

1. The first means simply "interval of time." Thus, when the master tells you "pass forward with your right foot and, in the same tempo, deliver a fendente," he means "deliver the fendente in the same interval of time as the forward passing step."

2. In other instances, it means "as a continued motion." Thus, when the master says "deliver a mandritto, and, in the same tempo, follow with a riverso," he means "deliver the two cuts without interruption." According to the Aristotelian physics commonly taught in Manciolino's day, time is the measure of uninterrupted motion between two instances of stillness, or of uninterrupted stillness between two motions.

3. Tempo also means "opportunity to attack," a fundamental component of Italian fencing theory. The Anonymous Bolognese states on page 20R, "In this art, as in skilled singing, the principal ability is knowing how to take tempi." Giovanni dall'Agocchie classifies five perfect instances to recognize a tempo in which to strike the opponent, which are also a rather common thread in Renaissance Italian swordsmanship (my comments in parenthesis):

    a. After parrying the opponent's attack.

    b. After the opponent's attack has fallen harmlessly out of your presence.

    c. While he lifts his hand to strike you (especially with a cut).

    d. While he changes guards without reason, and before he stops in the next.

    e. While he lifts his front foot (or if he passes forward).

Full and half tempo (*tempo intero* and *mezzo tempo*) – In simple terms, a full tempo is the time required for a full cut—for instance, one going from Guardia Alta to Porta di Ferro Larga. A half tempo is one required for a half cut, for instance, one going from Coda Lunga e Stretta to Porta di Ferro Stretta (please refer to the section on guards to see these positions).

Stance (*passo*)

Stance signifies primarily the distance between the feet, as well as the placement of the feet with respect to the line. As far as distance, this style employs both wide and narrow stances, as Manciolino's description of the guards makes amply clear. Manciolino also states that he favors a moderate stance; so, when others descriptions lack, I would opt to follow Manciolino's advice and keep the feet spaced approximately a half-arm's length apart. A stance can also be straight along the line (on-line stance), or oblique (off-line stance).

In general, we therefore have four kinds of stance:

Wide stance (*gran passo*) – This is a stance in which the feet are spaced farther apart—i.e., wider than a half arm's length.

Wide stance (shown with sword in Coda Lunga e Alta).

Narrow stance (*piccolo passo*) – This is the stance described, for instance, for the Guardia Alta, in which the feet are only a few fingers' widths apart.

Narrow stance (shown with sword in Guardia di Faccia).

Medium stance (*a pie' pari* or *passo giusto*) – This is, as Manciolino states, a stance in which the feet are not spaced "more than half an arm's length apart."

Medium stance (shown with sword in Coda Lunga e Alta).

Oblique stance (*passo largo*) – This is an off-line stance in which the feet are placed obliquely with respect to the line. For instance, in the description of the guard Cinghiara Porta di Ferro, the right rear foot is on the line, while the leading left foot is placed markedly to the left of the line.

Oblique stance, with the left foot to the left of the line (shown with sword in Cinghiara Porta di Ferro).

The issue of weight-distribution is also not conclusively addressed by swordsmanship treatises of this time. The earliest instruction we have in the matter comes at the beginning of the next century, and there is no good reason not to employ it for this style: keep the weight mostly on the foot that is not the next to move. Alternatively, keep it evenly distributed between the feet, especially when standing in a medium stance.

The Guards (Guardie)

No two Bolognese masters list the same exact number of guards, although there is a fair degree of consistency in how they describe the ones they have in common. Manciolino lists and describes ten main positions, and uses or references a handful more. In this section, I will provide the illustrations for the guards found in the only treatises of the time depicting most of them (Marozzo and Viggiani). Together with the description offered in the text, this is the best tool we have, to date, to know what the style looked like visually. I have also supplied photographs to illustrate the guards never depicted, namely the Guardia di Sotto il Braccio and the Guardia di Sopra il Braccio.

Bolognese guards are divided between high guards and low guards. We could say that high guards are the ones in which the sword hilt is at or above chest height, while the others are low guards. The low guards are further divided into Porta di Ferro (iron door) guards, featuring the sword-hand to the inside of the right knee, and Coda Lunga (long tail) guards, featuring the sword-hand to the outside of the right knee.

The high guards described or mentioned by Manciolino are Guardia Alta, Guardia di Testa, Guardia di Faccia, Guardia di Sopra il Braccio and Guardia di Sotto il Braccio (main guards) plus the Guardia di Alicorno. Among the low guards are the Porta di Ferro Stretta, Porta di Ferro Larga, Cinghiara Porta di Ferro, Coda Lunga e Stretta, Coda Lunga e Alta (main guards) plus Coda Lunga e Distesa and Coda Lunga e Larga.

Note: when the wide stance is listed, it is normally understood that a medium stance is also acceptable.

Guardia Alta

- Sword-hand above and to the right of the head, palm facing left
- Sword-point backward or at an angle high and backward
- True edge facing up
- Buckler extended forward at shoulder-height
- Stance: either narrow (right foot forward) or wide (either foot forward), feet in-line

Guardia di Testa

- Sword-hand at or just below shoulder-height, palm somewhat down
- Sword-point facing obliquely forward and to the left
- True edge facing forward
- Buckler extended forward at shoulder-height
- Stance: wide stance (either foot forward), feet in-line

Guardia di Faccia

- Sword-hand at face-height, to the inside and turned palm-up
- Sword-point pointing towards the opponent's face
- True edge facing left
- Buckler extended forward at shoulder-height, either facing forward or covering the sword-hand, but always close to the sword-hand
- Stance: wider or narrow (right foot forward) feet in-line

Guardia di Sopra il Braccio

- Sword-hand above the buckler arm (at elbow level), turned palm-down
- Sword point pointing backward
- True edge facing left
- Buckler extended forward at shoulder-height
- Stance: wide or narrow (right foot forward), feet in-line

Guardia di Sotto il Braccio

- Sword-hand under the buckler arm, turned palm-down
- Sword point pointing backward
- True edge facing left
- Buckler extended forward at shoulder-height
- Stance: wide or narrow (right foot forward) feet in-line

Note: the Sopra il Braccio and Sotto il Braccio are not only guards in which a swordsman can set himself. They are also transitory positions of the sword as it performs various actions, particularly cuts. Thus, for instance, if you perform a mandritto that goes Sopra il Braccio, you perform a mandritto in which the sword swings over your buckler arm. This is an important piece of data in the analysis of Manciolino's plays.

Guardia di Alicorno

- Sword-hand forward and to the right of the head
- Sword-point pointing left and obliquely towards the ground
- True edge facing up
- Buckler extended forward at shoulder-height
- Stance: wide (either foot forward) feet in-line

Guardia di Alicorno, divided by Marozzo as Guardia di Becha Possa (top) and Becha Cesa (bottom), depending on which foot leads.

Porta di Ferro Stretta

- Sword-hand at belt level and over or just to the left (inside) of the right knee, palm somewhat up and to the left

- Sword-point pointing at the opponent's face

- True edge facing down and to the left

- Buckler extended forward at shoulder-height

- Stance: wide (right foot forward), feet in-line

Porta di Ferro Larga

- Sword-hand at belt level and to the left (inside) of the right knee, palm somewhat up and to the left

- Sword-point pointing obliquely left and to the ground

- True edge facing down and to the left

- Buckler extended forward at shoulder-height

- Stance: wide (right foot forward), feet in-line

Cinghiara Porta di Ferro

- Sword-hand at belt level and to the left (inside of the right knee), palm somewhat up and to the left
- Sword-point pointing at the opponent's face
- True edge facing down and to the left
- Buckler extended forward at shoulder-height
- Stance: wide (left foot forward), oblique stance

Coda Lunga e Stretta

- Sword-hand at belt level, to the right (outside) of the right knee, the back of the hand facing somewhat up and to the right
- Sword-point pointing at the opponent's face
- True edge facing down and to the right
- Buckler extended forward at shoulder-height
- Stance: wide (right foot forward), feet in line

Coda Lunga e Alta

- Sword-hand at belt level, to the right (outside) of the right knee, the back of the hand facing somewhat up and to the right
- Sword-point pointing at the opponent's face
- True edge facing down and to the right
- Buckler extended forward at shoulder-height
- Stance: wide (left foot forward), feet in line

Coda Lunga e Larga

- Sword-hand at belt level, to the right (outside) of the right knee, the back of the hand facing somewhat up and to the right
- Sword-point pointing forward and to the ground
- True edge facing down and to the right
- Buckler extended forward at shoulder-height
- Stance: wide, feet in line

Coda Lunga e Distesa

- Sword-hand at belt level, held behind the person, palm facing right
- Sword-point pointing down and backward
- True edge facing down or down and to the left
- Buckler extended forward at shoulder-height
- Stance: wide, feet in-line

Footwork (Passeggiare)

Footwork in this style is perhaps the most varied in the history of Italian swordsmanship. It is also one of the most thoroughly described in pre-classical fencing treatises. However, a consistent terminology and a precise description of every form of step did not occur until much later. Because of this, modern teachers and students are coming to rely on a recently-created *lingua franca* that helps classify and explain all of the footwork in this style.

I will present the definition of each, offer a visual representation of what it looks like, and give examples of how the step is described in the text.

> **The pass (*passare*)** – A forward pass is when you advance by bringing your rear foot forward along the line. A backward pass is when you retreat by bringing your front foot backward along the line. The masters also use the term "pass" with reference to a step forward of either foot from a position where the feet are next to each-other or close to each-other in a narrow stance. In both cases, a pass is a single motion action, meaning that only one foot moves at one time.

Pass along the line (1): the fencers are lined up, in this case, with their right foot forward.

Pass along the line (2): the fencer on the left passes forward with his left foot, always along the line.

The oblique pass – An oblique pass is an off-line pass in which you bring your rear foot forward, but obliquely on the corresponding side of the line. Thus, a right oblique pass is when you bring your right rear foot forward to the right of the line. A left oblique pass is when you bring your left rear foot forward to the left of the line.

Oblique pass (1): the fencers are lined up.

Oblique pass (2): the fencer on the left passes with his left foot to the opponent's right side.

Note: in most early-16th-century treatises, the oblique pass is described as "pass with your right foot to the opponent's left" or "pass with your left foot to the opponent's right."

Note: the oblique pass is often followed by the compass step (see below for definition), so that the feet line themselves up on a new line (oblique pass and compass).

The cross-line pass – A cross-line pass is an off-line pass in which the rear foot passes forward while crossing the line. Thus, a right cross-line pass is when you bring your right rear foot forward to the left of the line. A left cross-line pass is when you bring your rear left foot forward to the right of the line.

Cross-line pass (1): the fencers are lined up.

Cross-line pass (2): the fencer on the left passes with his left foot across the line, i.e., to the opponent's left side.

Note: you will recognize the cross-line pass when Manciolino states (for instance), "pass with your right foot to the opponent's right."

Note: the cross-line pass is also occasionally followed by a compass step (cross-line pass and compass); it may also be followed by an additional pass, often in the same direction.

The accrescimento (*accrescimento*) – An accrescimento is a forward motion of the front foot along the line, which increases the distance between your feet. An accrescimento is also a single motion.

Accrescimento along the line (1): the fencers are lined up.

Accrescimento along the line (2): the fencer on the left executes an accrescimento along the line, i.e., steps forward with his front foot (in this case, the right).

The oblique accrescimento – This is an off-line accrescimento in which the leading foot proceeds obliquely on the corresponding side of the line. Thus, a right oblique accrescimento is one in which your forward, right foot steps obliquely to the right of the line. A left oblique accrescimento is one in which your forward, left foot steps obliquely to the left of the line.

Oblique accrescimento (1): the fencers are lined up.

Oblique accrescimento (2): the fencer on the left executes an oblique accrescimento, i.e., steps with his right foot to the opponent's left side.

The cross-line accrescimento – This is an off-line accrescimento in which the leading foot proceeds obliquely while crossing the line. Thus, a right cross-line accrescimento is one in which your forward, right foot steps obliquely to the left of the line. A left cross-line accrescimento is one in which your forward, left foot steps obliquely to the right of the line.

Cross-line accrescimento (1): the fencers are lined up.

Cross-line accrescimento (2): the fencer on the left executes a cross-line accrescimento, i.e., steps with his right foot to the opponent's right side.

Note: this step is also mostly defined in early-16th-century swordsmanship from the point of view of which side of the opponent you step towards: "step with your right foot to his right side," etc.

The compass step – This is a finishing step that often follows an off-line pass or off-line accrescimento. Its role is to realign the feet on a new line after performing oblique or cross-line footwork. It is performed by letting the rear foot describe an arc of a circle behind the leading foot, ending in such a way that the feet are in line with the opponent's center of mass. The compass step is a single motion.

Manciolino describes the step as "let your left foot follow behind the right" (left compass step) or "let your right foot follow behind the left" (right compass step).

Oblique pass and compass (1): the fencers are lined up.

Oblique pass and compass (2): the fencer on the left executes an oblique pass, in this case, with his left foot to the opponent's right side.

Oblique pass and compass (3): the fencer on the left finishes with a compass step, i.e., circles with his back-foot to end up with the feet along a new line. This finishing step can be executed after any off-line footwork, that is, oblique and cross-line passes and accrescimenti.

The gathering step – Besides the pass, the gathering step is the most used form of advancing and retreating footwork in early-16th-century Italian fencing. A forward gathering step consists of two motions: a) the forward gather, consisting of placing your rear foot close to your front foot; and b) the forward step, consisting of placing your front foot forward, thereby ending in the same-size stance as when you started. The backward gathering step also consists of two motions: a) the backward gather, consisting of placing your front foot close to your rear foot; and b) the backward step, consisting of placing your rear foot backward, thereby ending in the same-size stance as when you started.

Gathering step (1): the fencers are lined up.

Gathering step (2): the fencer on the left gathers forward with his rear foot, in this case, his left.

Gathering step (3): the fencer on the left steps forward with the foot that was forward, in this case, his right.

Note: since the second motion of a forward gathering step is an accrescimento, it may proceed on-line, obliquely or cross-line, as defined by the master.

Note: for a tradition with no living lineage, Bolognese footwork presents surprisingly few interpretation problems. The greatest exception is the potential confusion between a retreating backward pass and a mere gathering back of the front foot. For instance, the typical Italian *tirare il destro piede appo il sinistro* of such ambiguous passages is problematic because *appo* (also spelled *appoi*) can mean both "near" and "behind." Thus, these passages may mean "to pull the right foot near the left" as well as "to pull the right foot back behind the left." In some instances, the context clarifies which is correct; in others, I have deliberately left it open to interpretation. On the positive side, however, the tactical significance of either step is nearly identical, so performing either one generally makes the action correct.

The changed step (*cambio di piedi* or *passo cambiato*) – This step consists of two motions: a) gather back with your front foot; b) step forward with the other foot, either on- or off-line. The purpose is to switch which foot is forward.

Changed step (1): the fencers are lined up.

Changed step (2): the fencer on the left gathers back with his right foot.

Changed step (3): the fencer on the left steps forward with his other foot,
i.e., the left, thereby changing his stance from right- to left-foot-forward.

The backward jump (*salto* or *balzo indietro*) – This is a form of retreating footwork often found in Manciolino. It is never meticulously defined in the treatises, but we can assume it consisted of springing back with both feet leaving the ground at the same time, and returning on the ground some distance behind, in such a way that the relative position of the feet remains the same (unless otherwise specified by the master). The backward jump also consists of a single motion.

Backward jump (1): the fencers are lined up.

Backward jump (2): the fencer on the left jumps backward, with both feet leaving the ground at the same time.

Backward jump (3): the fencer on the left ends the jump with his feet on the ground
in the same stance as before the jump.

The Attacks (Offese): Moving Between the Guards

Angelo Viggiani states on page 76R and following that "every strike or motion lies between two guards (or instances of stillness), and every guard lies between two strikes." He adds, "we could even say that every action lies between two potentials and that every potential lies between two actions. A strike, while still enshrined in a guard, is not action but potential; when it is finally released, it becomes action."

This statement exemplifies how, in this style, strikes are simply forceful transitions between guards, with ideally as little departure from them as possible.

Strikes are divided between cuts and thrusts.

The Cuts (*Tagli*)

Cuts are attacks in which the shearing ability of the sword's edge is employed to inflict injury on the opponent. In general, they employ a simultaneous percussive and slashing (or slicing) element, the latter ideally involving as much of the debole as possible. The slicing element begins around the last third of the blade and proceeds towards the point; the exception is the pushed riverso, in which the cut begins closer to the point and proceeds towards the middle of the blade.

The common targets for cuts are the head or face, the sword-hand or sword-arm and the forward leg. Cuts to the body are rare—not only with the single-handed sword, but also with the *spadone* or two-handed sword, and with the polearms.

Cuts are classified in several ways: the general direction (*mandritto* or *riverso*), the specific path (*fendente*, *tondo*), the edge with which they are delivered (true- or false-edge cuts) and even whether they are executed in a wheel-like fashion (*stramazzone* and *mulinetto*).

Keeping it simple, here are the main cuts in the style and their definition. Note: all cuts are predominantly true-edge cuts unless otherwise defined here, or unless specified in the action described by the master.

Right-to-left cuts:

- Mandritto fendente: a true-edge cut proceeding downwards right-to-left, almost vertically.
- Mandritto squalembrato, or simply mandritto: a true-edge cut proceeding at a downward slant right-to-left.
- Mandritto tondo: a true-edge cut proceeding horizontally right-to-left.
- Mandritto ridoppio: a true-edge cut ascending at a slant right-to-left.
- Falso dritto: a false-edge cut having the same path as the mandritto ridoppio.

Vertical ascending cuts:

- Montante: a false-edge ascending cut proceeding vertically.

Left-to-right cuts:

- Riverso fendente: a true-edge cut proceeding downwards left-to-right, almost vertically.

- Riverso squalembrato, or simply riverso: a true-edge cut proceeding at a downward slant left-to-right.

- Riverso tondo: a true-edge cut proceeding horizontally left-to-right.

- Riverso ridoppio: a true-edge cut ascending at a slant left-to-right.

- Falso manco: a false-edge cut having the same path as the riverso ridoppio.

Other cuts:

- Stramazzone: a fendente-like cut delivered with a wheel-like motion of the wrist, with the sword turning to the left of the sword-hand.

- Mulinetto: a fendente-like cut delivered with a wheel-like motion of the arm (may be from the elbow or shoulder).

- Pushed riverso (*riverso spinto*): a riverso (most likely a tondo) in which the sword is pushed rather than pulled at the moment of impact; thus, the cut begins closer to the point and proceeds towards the middle of the blade.

The Thrusts (*Punte* or *Stoccate*)

Thrusts are offensive actions that use the penetrative power of the sword's point to inflict injury on the opponent.

In Bolognese swordsmanship, the most common targets for the thrust are the face, the chest and the flank.

Unlike how it is taught in later styles, the thrust in the Bolognese swordsmanship is often prepared by withdrawing the sword-hand, so that it may be delivered with a strong extension of the arm.

Following is the most common nomenclature for thrusts in the Bolognese style:

- Stoccata: a) a generic name for a thrust or b) an underhand thrust delivered with the false edge pointing up or pointing right.

- Imbroccata: an overhand thrust often proceeding downward.

- Punta dritta: a thrust executed with the hilt turned to the outside (the false edge pointing left) and directed more or less right-to-left.

- Punta riversa: a thrust executed with the hilt turned to the inside (the false edge pointing right) and directed more or less left-to-right.

- Punta in falso: an ascending thrust delivered with the false edge pointing up.

- Drilled thrust (*punta trivellata*): although this thrust is not strictly defined in extant treatises, it is most likely an underhand thrust accompanied by a quick turn of the hand at the moment of impact, achieving a drill-like effect.

Defense (DIFESE): Parries and the Role of the Buckler

A parry (*parata*) is a defensive action in which the sword (or main weapon) and/or the companion weapon is employed to thwart an incoming attack by a) beating it away, b) setting it aside or c) blocking its path. Sword-parries are performed with either the false or the true edge. Following are the most prevalent parries in Manciolino:

- The false-edge parry with a falso: this is a defensive action in which a falso cut or a montante is used to beat away the incoming attack. Like all cuts, it should employ the debole rather than the forte.

- The soft false-edge parry: more rarely, the false-edge parry calls for a softer setting aside rather than a dry beat. Note: Manciolino often uses the expression "parry with the false edge" indiscriminately to mean the falso parry in some cases and the soft false-edge parry in others. The context will suggest which parry to use.

- The false- or true-edge parry against attacks to the leg: this is a defensive action in which the sword, pointing down, stops the incoming attack with the false or true edge of the forte; the companion weapon should be covering the sword-hand.

Parrying a cut to the leg. Note how the buckler is used to cover the sword-hand (fencer on the left parrying). This parry may be executed with either edge (true-edge parry shown in this case).

- The true-edge parry: this is a defensive action in which the forte of the sword is employed to beat away, deflect or block an incoming attack. Most true-edge parries are performed in the following manners or a combination thereof:

    1. Through a beat or half cut. The half cut may be to the opponent's sword, to his hand or to his arm.

    2. With a *mezza volta* (see below for definition).

    3. By forming opposition, that is, an obtuse angle between the sword-arm and the sword.

    4. By getting into a guard, primarily the Guardia di Faccia and the Guardia di Testa.

Using the Guardia di Testa to parry a riverso to the head (fencer on the left parrying).

Using the Guardia di Faccia to parry a mandritto to the face (fencer on the left parrying). Please note how the buckler accompanies the sword in this parry, and how the sword-point is straightened towards the opponent's face to create a threat.

- The buckler parry—and other parries performed with shields, cape and (in most cases) the dagger—consist of conservative motions that minimize the risk of creating an opening between the arms.

    Note: in this style, the buckler has to be regarded as a piece of hand-held armor, as it were. It is practically never swung about in fast or large motions as it attempts to close lines or parry incoming attacks.

The Role of the Buckler

Let us take a quick survey of the main functions of the buckler, which is Manciolino's main companion weapon. For brevity's sake, I will omit discussion of the other particular companion weapons, also because their roles and uses are only partially dissimilar from those of the buckler. Here are the most common roles of the buckler, roughly listed in descending order of frequency:

- Closing the line of attack to your left by making the left side of your face and torso unavailable or outright invisible to the opponent. This is why, in all on-guard positions, it is important to hold the buckler-arm well extended towards the opponent: the closer your buckler is to him, the wider area of your body it will obscure.

- Protecting the sword-hand by covering it. In some instances, for example while going into Guardia di Faccia to thwart an attack to your face, the author will specify that the buckler has to be joined to the sword-hand. The actual position of the buckler is not detailed, but it should be so that the left hand directly touches the right (or the hilt of the sword, depending on how complex it is).

- Joining the sword-hand in various actions to close the center-line. This happens quite often in the actions of the half sword, when the master specifies that the buckler-hand needs to touch the sword-hand.

- Defending the head while the sword attacks the opponent's leg. This is by far the most common situation when the buckler is called upon to defend directly, rather than the sword. It does not require a large motion of the arm from the basic on-guard positions, but rather a small adjustment to your buckler-hand, so that the high line is unavailable to the opponent while you deliver your attack in the low line.

- Pushing on the opponent's sword, sword-hand or sword-arm, almost always while executing an action at the half sword. In these situations, the buckler is used to actively displace the opponent's weapon or arm, not unlike one would do in wrestling.

- Striking various parts of the opponent's body. This also occurs in the plays of the half sword, where the buckler may be used to directly inflict injury on the opponent—for instance, by striking his shin with the rim while he attempts to deliver a kick.

- Being hit with your own sword or pommel (*ritocco di brocchiero*). Striking your own buckler can have various reasons. For instance, quickly hitting the rim up and down (as in the main defenses against attacks from the Guardia Alta) serves to create a dynamic defense while ensuring that the weapons remain joined; in other instances, striking your own buckler can be part of an embellishment to the play, which, in turn, serves to add beauty to your game while unsettling the opponent.

- Providing the main defense against the opponent's attacks in other instances than the fourth point above. This occurs in a minority of situations, since the main defensive role of the buckler is to aid, rather than replace, the sword.

Other Actions and Definitions

The *mezza volta* with the sword-hand – A mezza volta (literally, "half turn") of the hand is the act of turning the hand from an inside, palm-up position to an outside, palm-down one—or vice-versa. Technically, it can also mean turning it from an overhand, palm-to-the-right position to an underhand, palm-to-the-left one, although most mezze volte occur along the inside-outside plane. A mezza volta may be done to change between guards (for instance, from Porta di Ferro or Guardia di Faccia to Coda Lunga), to parry, to provide strong opposition to a particular line, etc.

Mezza volta (1): the fencer lies with his sword in Coda Lunga.

Mezza volta (2): the fencer executes a mezza volta with his sword-hand, ending in Porta di Ferro. The mezza volta (executed to either side) may also be employed as a parry.

The mezza volta with the body – This, too, is a half-turn, but of the body instead of the hand. It is the act of turning your body from a chest-to-the-left to a chest-to-the-right position or vice-versa. Although it may be done by pivoting on the balls of the feet, the easiest way to effect this action is with a pass. For instance, if you have your left foot forward and your chest faces right, you can pass forward with your right foot and let your chest face left in an easy and natural manner. A mezza volta with the body may be performed to change guards or to change the perspective of the torso for tactical reasons.

Wide play (*gioco largo*) – This is the kind of play that involves wider distances, full cuts and whole tempi. Because it starts well out of measure, it admits the use of wide and high guards. It also calls for devices such as provocations and feints to unsettle the opponent, since starting at a wider distance also means that a stationary opponent has a better chance to react successfully. Stylistically, it should be performed as much as possible with the sword-arm well extended.[29]

---

[29]   See Anonymous Bolognese, p. 17 V.

Narrow play (*gioco stretto*, or *strette* of the half sword) – This is the kind of play that may start[30] after you and the opponent arrive at a crossing of the swords with neither of you having an advantage—meaning that either of you may initiate it. It occurs at shorter distances and involves half cuts and half tempi. Bolognese authors make it clear that this is a distinct type of play, often taught separately from the gioco largo.[31] Because it starts in a closer measure and it involves shorter tempi, it favors the use of guards that close the line (*guardie strette*) and that keep the point in-line, such as the Porta di Ferro Stretta and the Coda Lunga e Stretta. Also, it does not require provocations, but it admits simple attacks by cut or thrust, or compound attacks starting with a feint. Plays of gioco stretto may start in two ways:

- True edge on true edge, meaning from a true-edge crossing to the inside. Instances of actions leading to this crossing may include parrying an ascending punta riversa with your true edge, parrying a mandritto with a mezza volta from Coda Lunga, advancing against each other with the points in-line and the swords to the inside, etc.

The true-edge on true-edge position that may be used by either fencer
to enter the narrow play, or *strette*.

---

30 If, after a crossing, you do not wish to enter the gioco stretto, you may simply retreat one step and continue playing in the gioco largo.

31 One of the most interesting quotes in this regard comes from Marozzo, in chapter 162 of his *Opera Nova*. "Let's say there are two fencers, one of whom has learned both the wide and narrow play, while the other only knows the wide. The latter will be retreating his way through the salle, with the fencer who knows both plays chasing him around. This is why you should tell your students to learn both types of play, as long as they do not mind the payment. For the wide play with the two-handed sword (used against a similar weapon as well as against polearms) I charge seven Bolognese Pounds; for the narrow play (also used against a similar weapon as well as against polearms) I charge another seven, making it fourteen Bolognese Pounds total."

- False edge on false edge, meaning from a false-edge crossing to the outside. Instances of actions leading to this crossing may include parrying an ascending punta riversa or falso with your false edge, attempting a counterthrust to the outside, advancing against each other with the points in-line and the swords to the outside, etc.

The false-edge on false-edge position that may be used by either fencer
to enter the narrow play, or *strette*.

The gioco stretto or narrow play may involve sword-actions only, wrestling actions only, or a combination of the two.

Plays of *spada da gioco* – These are the plays taught with and for the practice sword, or *spada da gioco*. They are important because they contain all the elements of the art, including high, wide and low guards, full and half cuts, entries and returns from play, embellishments, etc. These plays may be telling vestiges of a tradition begun when armor was commonly worn, and they tend to disappear from Bolognese literature around the mid-1500s. Note: in one-handed sword, both Marozzo and Manciolino list the strette of the half-sword only as part of the plays of spada da gioco. Marozzo, however, also states that these can be performed with a variety of weapons and weapon-combinations including the sword with different shields, the sword alone, the two-handed swords and, in some cases, even the polearms.

Plays of *spada da filo* – These are the plays taught for (if not always with) the sharp sword or *spada da filo*. They are much more conservative than the plays of spada da gioco and tend to favor guards that close the line (*strette* guards) like the Coda Lunga and the Porta di Ferro. There is little or no use of high and wide guards, right-foot-forward positions are clearly favored, and the thrust assumes a much more prominent role than in the plays of spada da gioco. Although this is a gross oversimplification, we could say that the plays of spada da filo foreshadow the rapier fencing of the 1600s.

The Assalto and the Main Parts of the Play

The *assalto* appears to be the pedagogical centerpiece in the writings of Manciolino and his contemporary, Achille Marozzo. An assalto, to this day, is a fencing bout between two opponents. It is different from the *abbattimento*, which is actual combat. The difference in likely lethality is why, for instance, Marozzo tends[32] to call his plays of spada da gioco "assalti" and those of spada da filo "abbattimenti."

As it appears in the treatises of Marozzo and Manciolino, the assalto is a detailed sequence of several tens of actions that the student should memorize. The role of the opponent is only roughly sketched; this was most likely played by the instructor or a senior provost as the student learned and perfected his part.

As Manciolino says, the assalti "help make the body, the legs and the hands lively and quick. Therefore, he who does not take delight in stepping in tempo and in the way I will teach (and have taught), will enjoy neither grace nor victory in his fencing." The pedagogical importance of the assalto is that it contains the widest variety of actions—in other words, the greatest part of the art. Most actions in the Bolognese style can be found in the assalti of spada da gioco, while only a smaller variety of them find their way into the more conservative abbatimenti of the spada da filo.

Following is a list of the main components of Bolognese play. I have endeavored to list the most important parts of the assalti, and to detail which may be less likely to occur in the art of the spada da filo.

> **Entry into the play or access to the play (*andata di gioco*)** – This is a solo form or flourish that occurs most often at the beginning of the assalto of spada da gioco: the swordsman performs a series of steps synchronized with a series of blows until he halts a step or two out of measure from the opponent. None of the blows in this section are intended to reach the opponent, which is why Manciolino calls them "blanks" or "blows to the wind." The entry into the play also contains a cell of three or four steps called *abbellimento* or embellishment (see below), which will reappear throughout the play. The role of the entry into the play is to offer an interesting martial display to the opponent and to the spectators, as well as (undoubtedly) to warm up the limbs for the incoming bout.

> **Initial guard (*guardia*)** – Any play against the opponent begins in a specific guard, with a specific foot forward. This is true with both the spada da filo and the spada da gioco, as well as in all weapons and weapon-combinations.

> **Provocation (*provocazione*)** – This is an essential part of the gioco largo or wide play. It consists of an action designed to make your opponent move from his guard or force him to attack, thereby giving you a tempo in which to safely operate. Attacking a stationary opponent in the gioco largo without a provocation is dangerous and discouraged in this pragmatic, war-like style. Common types of provocations include the following:

---

[32] I say "tends" because, for instance, his second play of sword and targa is listed as both an assalto and an abbattimento, and even features a return from play.

- A simple advance with the sword pointed at the opponent.

- A thrust aimed at either side of his face.

- A falso or other cut to his sword-hand.

- A half cut or, more rarely, a cut.

- A cut or beat to the opponent's blade.

Attack (*ferita*) – After the provocation, if the opponent moves as desired, the actual, earnest attack may be launched. Attacks may be simple, with a feint, or redoubled.

- Simple attacks are earnest attacks consisting of one cut or one thrust and not preceded by a feint.

- Attacks with a feint are earnest attacks consisting of one cut or one thrust preceded by a feint. A feint is a simulated attack designed to draw a parry from the opponent that will be defeated by an earnest attack on a different line or target.[33] Most feints listed in the Bolognese style are single—i.e., one simulated attack; occasionally, the masters also list double feints—i.e., two simulated attacks executed without interruption.

- Redoubled attack: an earnest attack consisting of two or more blows. A redoubled attack may also be preceded by a feint (in this case, it becomes a redoubled attack with a feint). Because of its quick, wheel-like delivery, the stramazzone is often employed as the second or subsequent blow in a redoubled attack.

Parry (*parata*) – Almost always in Bolognese plays, a parry comes after an attack. Parries in the Bolognese style are almost always simple parries, meaning parries that do not contain a simultaneous counterattack. Some parries, however, such as the parry in Guardia di Faccia, place the point of the sword directly against the opponent's face, thereby putting some kind of burden of defense upon him.

Riposte (*risposta*) – After you are instructed to parry, you must deliver your riposte, which is an attack preceded by a parry. The riposte in the tempo immediately after the parry is a key part of the Bolognese style.

Embellishment (*abbellimento*) – This is a short flourish originally contained in the access to the play. It typically consists of three to five (mostly retreating) steps coordinated with sword blows and beats against your own buckler. Its role is to add grace to your play as well as to unsettle the opponent. Note: in Manciolino, embellishments occur only in the assalti of spada da gioco, where they may also serve as pedagogical breaks between the tens of actions of the assalto.

---

[33] There is an important difference between a provocation and a feint. A provocation is an action (not necessarily an attack) designed to either make the opponent move or to make him attack; a feint is a simulated attack always designed to provoke a parry.

Secondary attack and/or transition to the gioco stretto – After the provocation, the cycle between attack, parry and riposte can repeat itself more than once. Also, in the assalti of spada da gioco it can happen that there is a momentary transition into the strette of the half sword; in Manciolino, this usually occurs after an embellishment, whereby the sword is lowered from Guardia Alta in various ways, crossed with the opponent's and brought to bear in an action of gioco stretto.

Defensive retreat – After one or more cycles of attacks, parries and ripostes, the masters advise performing a defensive retreat consisting of one or more retreating steps or a backward jump, while the sword executes actions designed to defend you and keep the opponent at bay. There is no specific period term for a defensive retreat, the masters simply say "for your safety, retreat by..." and then detail the action to be performed.

Return from play (*ritorno di gioco*) – This is the opposite of the entry into the play: a series of retreating steps and synchronized sword blows and flourishes that bring you away from the opponent while offering an interesting martial display to him as well as those watching. Like the entry into the play, this section does not contain blows that are meant to reach the opponent.

Attitude and Mental Disposition In Bolognese Swordsmanship

"How beautiful this art becomes when it is adopted by four chief Virtues, which are courage, cunning, strength and agility!"[34] This sentiment, voiced by the Anonymous Bolognese, is part of a long dissertation he makes on the mental aspect of fencing the student should adopt. The attitude one brings to swordsmanship influences the way he fences and gives a measure of the person's character.

In his introductory section on general rules and advice to the reader, Manciolino also gives us a sense of how, in his day, the outward appearance of the style was seen as both a complement to one's own martial skills and a likely window on one's inner disposition and virtues (or lack thereof). This is reinforced by many other examples in period literature—both martial and peaceful. Among these, I have thought it best to offer the reader what I consider to be the most telling example, which is found in the Anonymous Bolognese.

Writing after presenting the most important definitions concerning the guards and steps, the offenses and defenses, and the types of play, the Anonymous moves on to the mental aspect of the style (p. 13R and following).

---

[34] In Italian, *animo, ingegno, forza* and *destrezza*. These are quite similar to the four virtues named by Italian master Fiore de' Liberi on page 32R of his treatise *Fior di Battaglia*, which are caution, speed, courage and strength (*avvisamento, prestezza, ardimento* and *fortezza*).

"I'll say that if you aim for the honor of expertise in this art, you need to prepare yourself in the way I describe. First, you need to adopt a high degree of attention to detail and perseverance. Attention to detail and perseverance must come with much toil. Toil must come with a good deal of patience. Patience must come with love of the art, which cannot materialize without understanding. Understanding requires grasping the reasons behind the art, and these require support, which in turn requires intellect and prudence. Prudence must come with knowledge. Once you attain this prudence and knowledge, your judgment will be that of an expert.

"If you cultivate or follow the highly-ingenious art of fencing (or art of arms), you must make sure that as you acquire the aforementioned virtues, you are totally devoid of fear.[35] It is quite obvious that the fearful will never win a battle or be crowned in victorious triumph. The roots of trees that produce unjust, poisonous branches and fruits never yield good refreshment.

"The proper feeling for this art is one that knows no humility, caring displays, nor mercy, niceties, inanity or laziness. If you were to keep any of these alive in you and persevered in niceties and lovely meekness, you would lose honor and gain shame to a high degree. So, you must first rid yourself of fearful thoughts and actions, or other traces of what produces anxiety. These thoughts and actions do not contain the virtues required in a manly and formidable fight, since if you become a slave to these feelings, you are like the dew in the sun or like a fable with no moral.

"All should regard this art as not needing the feelings I have just mentioned, which is quite the opposite from the virtues that normally embellish a person as precious stones are mounted on unmixed gold. Likewise, in fencing, you must be virgin-pure from any hint or whiff of fear, and of any negative mental image. The true virtue of this art consists in being intimidating, and in possessing such ferocity as to appear to be on fire, with fierceness and absolute mercilessness in your countenance. Every slightest motion you make must exude a craving for delivering cruel blows; when you approach the opponent with such fierceness, you will completely wipe out his self-possession.

"Move in such a way as to give him the impression that every gesture from you carries the potential for inflicting a crippling wound. Make your attacks so cruel and violent that even the slightest blow is enough to fill the opponent with dread. In this art, you need to act and have the countenance of the cruelest of lions or the angriest of bears. Actually, it wouldn't be a bad thing if you could make yourself look like a great devil and act like you wanted to whisk away his soul."

And *Great Devil* is just what a famous man who fenced this style came to be known.

---

[35] Quite understandably, this was a common theme in fencing treatises of the period. For instance, an often-quoted passage from the late-medieval German tradition admonishes the potential student that if he is easily frightened, he will not learn fencing (Erschrickstu gern / kain vechten nÿmmer gelerñ—Von Danzig, p. 3V).

Giovanni dalle Bande Nere, the Great Devil: A Portrait of a Famous Swordsman of the Bolognese Style

Portrait of Giovanni de' Medici, or Giovanni dalle Bande Nere, c. 1559 based on earlier portraits taken from life –
Palazzo Vecchio, Florence.

Note: Bolognese master Angelo Viggiani lists a number of famous noblemen and military lead-ers of his time who fenced in the style we call "Bolognese." Among them (p. 73R) is Giovanni de' Medici, also known as Giovanni dalle Bande Nere (Giovanni of the "Black Bands"), who Viggiani tells us was particularly fond of the guard Porta di Ferro Stretta. This is a short sketch to give the students of the sword a sense of the men who used this style of fencing. For more information on Giovanni, please refer to the bibliography at the end of this section.

Forlì', 1488. Countess Caterina Sforza looked over the parapet of the besieged citadel. Below, among the multitude of armed men and horses, stood the leaders of the Orsi family, eager for conquest. These men had just ransacked her house, murdered her husband, and were now threatening to do the same with her three children, unless she give up the citadel. "Open the gate, or we cut their throats! Right here, in front of you, one by one," shouted one man, who held a dagger at the neck of Caterina's eldest.

A brief pause. All was still, except for a warm spring breeze. Then she moved. She climbed three steps to the top of the parapet. Her voice rang like a bronze bell to the men below, "do as you please." With a jaunty move, she swept up the fine fabrics of her gown and sneered: "Can't you see I have the perfect mold to make more?"

Mere days later, *la Tigre* (the tigress) had saved the citadel, rescued her children and visited the most frightful revenge on the conspirators.

It was from such fire that, ten years later, Giovanni was born. Born from fire, living in fire, and dying by fire; he was one of the most celebrated generals of the Renaissance, among the last of the condottieri and perhaps the best swordsman of his day.

Giovanni was born in April 1498 from Caterina Sforza and Giovanni di Pierfrancesco de' Medici, a politician from the cadet branch of the Medici family who died shortly after his son's birth. Little Giovanni (*Giovannino*) spent his early years fleeing his powerful mother's enemies. Caterina, however, took special care to see him educated and to let him acquire the best swordsmanship and horsemanship skills—skills that he eagerly internalized and perfected until they defined him.

In 1509, Caterina died, but not before recommending Giovanni to the Salviatis, a rich and influential Florentine family who gladly took him as a ward—and whose meek-mannered daughter, Maria, instantly fell for him and eventually married him. Giovanni, however, soon revealed that his disposition was not one for calm family life. He was a man of the sword, first and foremost.

In those days, there was a famous young man in Florence, by the name of Boccaccino Alamanni. They said he was the best swordsman in town. This rumor was enough to provoke the adolescent Giovanni, who simply had to measure himself against this man. In the ensuing swordfight, those present placed all the odds in favor of Boccaccino, bracing themselves for the inevitable lesson that his impudent challenger would receive. Yet, with flawless skill and fiery temperament, Giovanni averted all of Boccaccino's attacks, and in a perfectly-timed rush of his own delivered a powerful sword-stroke to the opponent's head, leaving him at the edge of death. This victory may have won Giovanni early fame, but it also cost him a temporary banishment from the town of Florence.

Only a few years later, Giovanni was in Rome, cementing that relationship of mutual trust with Pope Leo X that was to propel him into a dazzling military career. When not at the papal court, Giovanni spent time with swordsmanship and with women; but it was at this point that he made the wrong conquest, a girl of the Orsini family, a proud Roman dynasty whose position demanded this affront be washed in blood.

Giovanni and a handful of friends were ambushed on the bridge of Castel Sant'Angelo by a large number of men from the Orsini family. This fight was immortalized posthumously by Giorgio Vasari, in a fresco found in Florence's *Palazzo Vecchio*. We see the young man with a two-handed sword, his body fully twisted over his feet as he swings great cuts and threatens powerful thrusts at the numerous opponents, over whom he prevailed, even killing a military captain who was his rival.

Giovanni was no less skilled on the battlefield. Not even eighteen years old, he successfully underwent his baptism of fire in a quickly-resolved war against the city of Urbino. One of Giovanni's greatest military gifts was the ability to instantly recognize the critical elements that won or lost battles, and implement revolutionary changes in his own forces.

He identified the growing weakness of heavy cavalry in the age of gunpowder. Mobility and speed, he thought, were cavalry's greatest assets, thereby giving his men smaller, lighter and faster Turkish and Berber horses. He saw that training and uniforms had to be of high quality and consistent—in an age when individualism and eccentricity were the trademark of the man-at-arms. He therefore personally oversaw the training of his men, and dictated that all (himself included) outfit themselves in plain uniforms, similar to one-another. He also placed a great emphasis on *esprit de corps*, sharing his men's privations and difficulties, but expecting absolute loyalty in return: defectors and traitors met a sure death.

After the passing of his beloved mentor, Pope Leo X, Giovanni ordered his troops' armor to be burnished black, as a sign of mourning. The collateral effect of this was to make his army even more feared: Giovanni had become *Giovanni dalle Bande Nere*, or Giovanni of the Black Bands.

Between 1523 and 1524, he was at the service of the imperials against the French. He humiliated the forces of the famed captain Bayard,[36] and routed the indomitable Swiss infantry at Caprino Bergamasco. To his enemies, he seemed unstoppable, earning the frightening nickname of *Il Gran Diavolo*, the great devil. But to Pope Clement VII (a Medici Pope), he had become too powerful—and inconvenient. Giovanni was an upstart, the Pope thought, and, worse, one from a rival branch of the family.

When King Francis I descended from France in 1524—this time with a huge army—and quickly took Milan, the Pope saw himself threatened by two forces: Emperor Charles V, with his vast army of Spaniards, Italians and German mercenaries on one side, and the French on the other. The Pope bet on the French; as a placating gesture of sorts, he decided to put Giovanni and his men at their service.

The French were immediately impressed with Giovanni. And Giovanni was immediately unimpressed with the French, and their indecision, and the great cavaliers making up their high command. In one particular instance, Giovanni was sitting impatiently in a generals' meeting; the purpose was to find ways to reduce a fortified post stubbornly held by the imperials. Of the generals who spoke, it seemed that the incompetent ones had the loudest voices, while the worthy ones kept silent, as did Giovanni. Until it all became unbearable to

---

[36] Pierre Terrail LeVieux, seigneur de Bayard (1473–30 April 1524), was a French soldier, generally known as the Chevalier de Bayard, and "the knight without fear and beyond reproach" (*le chevalier sans peur et sans reproche*). However, he himself preferred the name given him by his contemporaries for his gaiety and kindness, *le bon chevalier*, or "the good knight." His campaign in Italy, where he clashed with Giovanni, proved to be his last. He was killed by an arquebus ball while guarding the rear during the French retreat at Sesia.

him. Suddenly, he stood up, roaring "enough with words: it is action we need," and left. The meeting was still in progress when Giovanni stepped back into the room with the news that he had captured the position.

Burial harness of Giovanni dalle Bande Nere – Museo Stibbert, Florence.

By now, Giovanni was a legend. Great Italian minds like Machiavelli, author of *The Prince* and *The Art of War* and satiric poet Pietro Aretino (known as "the scourge of princes," for he could destroy the reputation of the powerful with a handful of verses) were his intimate friends and devout followers. When, after a number of serious French setbacks, a league was proposed in defense of Italy, Giovanni seemed the only logical choice to lead it: Giovanni, with his elite Black Bands, should be at the head of a league comprising the Vatican, France, Venice and Florence, in defense of Italy against the aggressor Charles V. For the first time in centuries, all the great powers of Italy would unite against a common enemy. The problem was that the Pope had to agree to place Giovanni in command—Giovanni the upstart, Giovanni from the "wrong" branch of the family. In the way of all great tragedies, family rivalry and personal ambitions trumped the greater good; so this was never to be.

Thus, Giovanni was made a general in the league, but not the supreme commander. And whenever he could, Pope Clement saw to it that Giovanni would be sent to the front lines, hopeful that his daring would lead to his undoing sooner rather than later. Pay for his men was often deliberately delayed, and Giovanni's wife Maria warmly pleaded to her husband to be careful and to see the Pope's betrayal for what it was. Still, Giovanni kept distinguishing himself on the field and, even after receiving a severe bullet wound to the leg, kept leading his Black Bands to victory.

And then, one day, it happened. Writes Aretino, "as the hour drew near when the Fates, with the consent of God, had decreed the end of our lord, his Dignity was making haste with the customary gallantry towards Governolo, where the enemy had entrenched. In the course of a skirmish around the town's kilns, behold! a falconet strikes him (alas) in that same leg that had been already wounded by an arquebus."

"And so it went; as the breath of his comrades' lamentations warmed the flakes of snow falling profusely from the sky, our lord was carried in a stretcher to Mantua and into the house of Lord Luigi Gonzaga."

There would be no miraculous second recovery. In the company of his loving friend Aretino, he quickly agreed to have his leg amputated, as the gangrene was spreading fast. After an excruciating operation, during which he himself held the candle for the surgeons, Giovanni seemed indomitable: he would go back to the battlefield and "teach those Germans how to fight and how to taste vengeance."

Things, however, took an inexorable turn for the worse. In agonizing pain, he asked Aretino to lull him to sleep by reading to him, which his friend eagerly did, tears in his eyes. When he sensed that his soul was finally yielding to darkness, Giovanni asked for and received the sacrament of extreme unction, then uttered his last words: "I don't want to die amidst all these medical paraphernalia." He was carried outside, and died on a soldier's cot on November 30, 1526. He was 28 years old.

Writes Aretino in prophecy: "And Florence, and Rome (please, God, let me be lying!) will soon get a taste of a world without him. I am already hearing the cries of the Pope, who believes to have gained by the loss of our lord."

Now free from their main military obstacle, the imperial forces descended on Italy and, six months later, brutally sacked Rome, forcing the Pope into hiding, and writing one of history's most ignominious pages.

Bibliography

Mario Scalini (ed.), *Giovanni dalle Bande Nere*, Silvana Editoriale, 2001

Joseph J. Deiss, *Captains of Fortune*, Crowell, New York, 1966

Aretino, Pietro, *Lettere*, Edizioni Carocci, Rome, 2000

G. de' Rossi, *Vita di Giovanni de' Medici*, Rome, 1996

F. Guicciardini, *Storia d'Italia*, Mazzali, Milano, 1988.

A Note on Language, the Translation, and on Editorial Decisions

Manciolino's treatise is elegantly written. It reveals a cultured author with a rather heightened artistic sensibility, and certainly aware of style and of the norms of good writing. He composes, essentially, in two styles: the plain style for the body of his instruction (as it is to be expected) and a more elevated style for the introductory chapters, sometimes used earnestly, other times bordering on the self-ironic. Manciolino is extremely careful not to mix instruction with the topic of his introductions—both stylistically and from a content standpoint.

My translation mirrors this dualism and the different shades in tone and voice, as much as it is possible in the new language. The translation will mostly come across as a newly-composed work, since this is how the original Italian reads; the only archaisms and poetic licenses are found in the introductions, which I have attempted to mirror in voice and style as faithfully as possible in English.

Now, a few words on the technical content. In most swordsmanship treatises, there are three kinds of terminology:

1. Strictly established technical terms pertaining only to swordsmanship. These have few or no parallels in everyday spoken language; examples are *mandritto*, *riverso*, *stramazzone*, the various names of the guards, etc.

2. Words or expressions that are part of the everyday Italian lexicon and that have virtually identical meaning in every context; examples are *right hand*, *left hand*, *forward*, *backward*—as well as connective speech such as *if the opponent attacks you, then...*, etc.

3. Words or expressions that are both technical fencing terms and have a meaning in the ordinary spoken language; examples are *to pass*, *tempo*, *opening*, *mezza volta*, *inside*, *outside*, *risposta* ("riposte" in fencing and "answer" in everyday language), *schifare* ("to parry" in fencing and "to avoid" in everyday language), etc. These may also be technical terms that were not yet fully standardized and established at the time of the treatise's writing, and thus may appear under different synonyms.

In translating, the only terms that present potential problems are those in the third category, since, without knowing this style of swordsmanship, it would be easy to mistake their technical meaning for that used in everyday speech. This is made more complicated by the fact that they often appear under different synonyms, due to the lack of standardization that some of them have in Manciolino's period. This is why it is important to cross-reference one treatise with the others of its tradition, as has been done in this case.

I have made a great effort to ensure that the semantics of the translation are an accurate representation of those in the original. Whenever pertinent, I have added footnotes to further clarify the meaning of a passage, or to point out the few obvious mistakes and clerical errors present in the original. I have also footnoted other passages, such as some of the allusions to myth and philosophy, to make the reading experience richer and more enjoyable.

The most substantial editorial decision has been to break up the long lists of actions into more manageable bullet points whenever practical and possible. This will make it considerably easier for the modern reader to grasp Manciolino's instructions and to follow his actions, sword-in-hand. This decision has not affected the accuracy of the translation either linguistically or semantically.

In all, I hope this translation and the accompanying compendia will help advance the interest in Bolognese swordsmanship and the understanding of this important martial tradition. I also hope that the author of the earliest-extant, printed Italian fencing book will receive a much-deserved boost in popularity, since his concise but amazingly thorough treatise describes the skills of the complete Renaissance swordsman.

OPERA NOVA

By Antonio Manciolino, Bolognese

*Containing the explanations and the advantages that
can be obtained in the use of any sort of arms;
newly revised and printed.*

1531

To the most illustrious Don Luigi de Cordoba, Duke of Sessa, Ambassador of the Most Serene Emperor to Adrian VI[37]

I llustrious Duke—Many a knowledgeable and excellent author, worthy of immortal praise have striven to impart instruction to their contemporaries through live teachings, as well as to posterity and to their progeny. Yet, until our times (as far as we know), nobody but the present author has explained in writing how to defend against a knowledgeable opponent, if attacked. In the short work that follows, the author attempts to teach how to avoid and elude cruel, violent death, as Your Illustrious Lordship will see in this brief book that bears a dedication to You. To You, as a Captain most expert in the art of arms; to You, whose brow so frequently bore the Laurel of victory. Aye, so small a book goes to so great a man; but please regard the spirit and the intent of a someone who is prepared to do anything for him who God may make perfect, and whom God may keep safe from adverse fortune. Be well.

---

[37] Don Luis Fernandez de Cordoba (1480–1526) was Duke of Sant' Angelo, Count of Cabra—and Duke of Sessa upon his marriage to Elvira de Cordoba y Figueroa, hereditary daughter of the famous captain Gonzalo Fernandez de Cordoba. A rather well-known military man who was in line to be nominated Captain General of the Neapolitan army, Don Luis reluctantly left the battlefield to end his life as a diplomat. In October 1522, in fact, the Spanish ambassador to the Holy See, Don Juan Manuel, relinquished his post and recommended Don Luis as his successor. In September 1523, Pope Adrian VI died and a month later, Don Luis was made knight of the Golden Fleece. After his wife's death in 1524, a heartbroken Don Luis asked Charles to be relieved of his post as ambassador, and died in Rome in August 1526. This dedication, as well as the words "newly revised and printed" point to the fact that the first edition of the *Opera Nova* must have seen the light between October 1522 and October 1523.

OPERA NOVA TO LEARN
How to Fight and Defend with any Sort of Arms, Written by Antonio Manciolino, Bolognese

It is customary among the commonest teachers of our art, that reason-based warden against injury, to place long stretches of paper in the highest and noblest part of their salle, bearing (they say) the principles of their instruction. Certainly, he who reads these banners will find they contain principles; however, these instructors, acting as wine-merchants do with their barrels, operate more monstrously than humanly.

And how could such behavior be human, when it patently reveals the insatiable greed of the teacher? As it is a human virtue to be of service to others and to admit that nobody is self-generated, so I believe it is steely greed to place in a school what is there only for one's own benefit instead of that of others. Such are the principles of the aforementioned teachers, who do nothing but sell at a price the noble plays of our art, as if the Virtue of Arms had fallen into such a low state to spur some to brag about peddling her sacred limbs in schools. These men do not see that a blunt mind cannot be yoked alongside a sharp intellect; and that the Art is not a whore to be sold at a price.

Wanting to take the more useful path, I declare that schools should have as a purpose the teaching of the Art; through this work, I am more gratified to be of service to my students than to derive great benefits by selling fencing principles at a price.

All I ask from my students are three things: respect, faith and remuneration. Respect because I am their teacher; faith because (as the Philosopher says) it is something a student owes his Master; and just remuneration because (as Cicero wrote) it is something without which the arts would wither. If I can call myself satisfied on these three points, why waste additional time on anything else, while I can do some good with this work?

HERE BEGIN A FEW
Main Rules or Explanations
on the Valiant Art of Arms

I f you want to fence with someone, seek to do so with those most skilled in deeds and in reputation. As the glory of the victor depends on the valor of the vanquished, so is a loss beyond reproach if it is embellished by the reputation of the winner.

Getting used to fence with various and diverse opponents will make you cunning, prudent and swift-handed: it is from the variety of so many active minds that comes that wise and refined Mother we call Experience.

While you and your opponent are studying each-other, never stop in a particular guard, but change immediately from one guard to the next. This will make it harder to judge your intentions.

There are fencers who deliver their attacks with great force, which tends to intimidate the opponent. Against those, you can do two things. The first is to let his blow pass and feint a parry and carefully push your own attack; the second is to rush forward and parry before his attack gains momentum. You could also hit him in the hand, which would make him forget his forceful attacks.

Just as striking the opponent's hand is [not][38] counted as a hit in a friendly match, (as the hand is the foremost exposed limb), in a real encounter this type of strike would be most effective. The part of the opponent's body you should attack the most is that with which he performs most attacks on you—namely, the hand.

The most admirable of all blows is the mandritto, because it is the most virtuous and noble, since it is more dangerous and awkward to perform. Using the mandritto is more dangerous than using the riverso because it causes you to be completely uncovered in that tempo—this is why it is deemed more noble.

Always keep an eye on the opponent's sword-hand rather than his face. By looking at his hand, you will be able to devise all that he intends to do.

---

[38] The word "not" (*non*) found in this sentence is placed right between "opponent's" and "hand" and this misplacement could very well be a clerical or typographical error, in which case it should be ignored. If, instead, the "non" stands, the meaning of the sentence would slightly change to signify that although a hit to the hand is not counted in play, it would constitute a crippling attack in a real fight.

The skillful parrying of a blow is of no little profit or beauty, and can be of equal or greater elegance than a good attack. Many are able to deliver good blows, but few have the skill to parry them (without getting hit) to the satisfaction of those watching.[39]

It is necessary to develop the knowledge of tempi, without which your fencing will remain imperfect. Therefore, let me advise you that as the opponent's attack has passed outside your presence, this is the correct tempo in which to follow with the riposte you deem most appropriate.

Near-sighted fencers should carry shorter swords, since their skill would not extend to a longer weapon.

In general, carrying a shorter weapon or a shorter sword shows greater skill, because it forces fencers to be closer; this, in turn, forces them to become good at parrying and develops their reflexes.

For many reasons, it is most advisable to learn all sorts of weapon-play with either hand, and to develop the ability to strike and parry with the right or the left hand.

We have both high guards and low guards. The objective of the high guards is to attack and then to follow with a parry; that of low guards is the opposite—to parry first and then to follow with a strike. Be advised that from the low guards only thrusts are natural attacks.

Just as you should not strike without parrying, you should not parry without striking—always observing the correct tempi. If you were to always parry without striking, you would make your timidity plain to your adversary, unless you were to push the opponent back with your parry, in which case you would show your valor. Correct parries, in fact, are performed going forward and not backward; in this manner, you can not only reach your opponent,[40] but you will also attenuate his blow against you, as from close by the opponent can only strike you with the part of the sword from mid-blade to the hilt; much worse it would be if he were to reach you with the other half of the sword.

An opponent who keeps retreating will cause your skills to lose their luster, since you will be unable to perform any good techniques against someone who flees constantly. Therefore, you should yourself pretend to flee your opponent, which will give him the courage to come forward; this will cause your fencing to recover its lost elegance.

Fencers who deliver many blows without any measure or tempo may indeed reach the opponent with one of their attacks; but this will not redeem them of their bad form, being the fruit of chance rather than skill. Instead we call *gravi & appostati*[41] those who seek to attack their opponent with tempo and elegance.

---

[39] This and many other sentences in Manciolino give us a sense of how the elegant display of skills was just as important in this art as sheer effectiveness. This goes to reinforce the thesis of those who believe that these arts were indeed perceived as such and not merely as pragmatic self-defense tools. And this is indeed consistent with the lengthy dissertation on the role that elegant fencing played in the education of the *Uomo Universale* presented by Castiglione in his *Cortegiano*.

[40] For the counterattack.

[41] *Grave* means, in this case, composed in his control and mature in his actions. *Appostato* means consciously observing the right posture and tempo.

If you are near your opponent, you should never swing a full blow,[42] because your sword should never get out of presence for your own safety. The delivery of these half-blows[43] is called *mezzo tempo*.

If you and your opponent are of equal knowledge of the Art and neither can safely deliver an attack to the other, I advise that you take a chance in your hope for victory. You can either rely on your reflexes and attack in the same tempo as your opponent, or you can strike him wherever you can and immediately spring against him and put your arms around him.[44] By doing this, everyone will judge you the victor.

If you are trying to make the opponent deliver an attack in order to strike him within that same tempo, you should yourself deliver the same attack three or four times in a row, almost as an invitation. It is common among fencers to ape one-another, so your opponent will see himself compelled to eventually do the same to you; and in that moment you will perform the attack as planned.

If you want to strike your opponent in his upper body, you should begin your action below; similarly, if you want to strike him below, you should begin your operations above. This is because as one defends the parts being attacked, he necessarily creates openings elsewhere.

Since no blow can be reasonably performed without ending in a guard, the virtue of a fencer is to be found in the raising and lowering of the guards.[45] In consequence of this principle, he who renews his attack before settling in guard will be more apt to win. This is because it is easier to attack an opponent whose action is interrupted.

As you parry on whichever side, always keep your arms well-extended. By doing so, you not only push the opponent's attacks away from your person, but you are also stronger and quicker in striking him.

By practicing with heavy weapons and learning to deliver long and extended blows, you will develop good stamina and excellent strength.[46] Afterwards, as you fight with lighter weapons you will find yourself a lot more agile.

---

[42] *Colpo Finito*. This is a cut which swings all the way past the target.

[43] *Colpo Imperfetto*. Literally meaning "unfinished blow," it does not create the drawbacks of a *colpo finito* by virtue of not letting the sword exit the presence. See also Viggiani for similar comments. The documented concept goes back to Filippo Vadi, who tells us to always parry with a blow so that our point stands at the opponent's breast and face. Elsewhere, he tells us to frame our blows the same way. Even earlier, Fiore hints at this by saying that all blows and thrusts reach their completion in posta longa, but he then clearly follows through to another guard.

[44] This technique is similar to the common one seen even today in modern wrestling and boxing, where one "hugs" the opponent to put it out of his power to move his arms.

[45] *Montare e callare delle guardie*. It is to be remembered that guards are divided into high and low and that, therefore, as one switches between them, the sword is raised and lowered.

[46] This piece of advice is consistent with that given to us by Alfieri but at odds with the instructions of Di Grassi, who prefers practicing with lighter weapons in order to develop speed.

In the Art of the *spada da filo*,[47] you should not depart from the low guards, because they are safer than their high counterparts. The reason is that when you are in a high guard you can be reached by a thrust or a cut to the legs, while in a low guard this danger does not exist.

Those who learn how to parry the opponent's blows with the false edge of the sword will become good fencers, since there can be no better or stronger parry than the ones performed in this manner.

While fighting or fencing, never let the opponent win by overwhelming you with his blows or with his audacity; doing so would deprive you of your courage and give it to the opponent instead.

Fencing with sword alone is much more profitable than any other weapon, since you are seldom without your sword. While you do not have your *rotella*[48] or buckler with you at all times, your sword can always be at your side.

As you fence a left-handed opponent, walking continuously towards his sword is an excellent defense. As he delivers a riverso, throw a mandritto to his sword-hand; when he delivers a mandritto, give him a riverso to the sword-hand or sword-arm. This technique will give you certain victory.

Although it is undoubtedly useful and beneficial to walk[49] with one or the other foot (depending on the tempo or the occasion) as you fence, I personally think that it is preferable to always walk even-footed, since doing so will allow you to extend forward and get back without disordering your body. Also, let me add that walking in this manner will keep you stronger than doing so in any other fashion. When I say "even-footed" I mean in such a way that the feet are never more than half an arm's length apart, and that the foot and the hand always accompany each other.[50]

Nobody can be deemed perfect in this art (as well as in others) unless he can impart his knowledge to others. As the Philosopher said in the *Ethics*,[51] the mark of the expert is the ability to teach.

---

[47] Manciolino intends a weapon with an actual edge as opposed to a practice sword. *Filo* is Italian for "edge."

[48] The *rotella* is a larger round shield common in swordsmanship treatises of the time. Generally, it has a diameter of 20"–36" and it features two leather arm-straps instead of the smaller buckler's solid, single handle. The *rotella* continued to be used and taught by Italian masters alongside the rapier all the way into the 17th-century.

[49] *Passeggiare.* This can be interpreted simply as "walking" or, more specifically, as "passing." Below, *passeggiare a pie' pari* is translated to "walking even-footed." Manciolino's own explanation of the phrase occurs at the end of the paragraph.

[50] This "agreement of hand and foot" was still being repeated as a fundamental principle by Giacomo di Grassi, three generations later.

[51] Aristotle's *Nicomachean Ethics,* whose foundations permeated European education until recent times.

As you fence with the two-handed sword in the *gioco largo*, keep your eye on the part of the opponent's sword from half-blade to the tip. However, once you are at the half-sword, you should look at your opponent's left hand, since it is with it that he may come to grapples.[52]

The art of the half-sword is necessary to the curriculum of anyone who wishes to become a good fencer. If you were only skilled in the *gioco largo*, and found yourself in the *stretto*, you would be compelled with shame and danger to pull back, thus often relinquishing victory to your opponent—or at least betraying your lack of half-swording skills to those who watch.

If you find yourself fencing a stronger and more powerful opponent, you should by all means avoid coming to grapples, since in that case, you will be forced to lose as the weaker of the two.

If the choice of weapons is given to the stronger of the two combatants, he should arm the weaker opponent heavily; although reason suggests that the less strong be given lighter arms and armor.[53]

If a large person is to fight a small one and the choice of weapons is granted to the former, he should elect to arm the lower body and not the upper. In this manner, he will find it easier to hit the opponent there by virtue of his greater size. Conversely, if the choice of weapons was given to the smaller of the two, he should elect to arm the upper body and leave the lower body unarmored.

Opponents of equal skill, strength and size can either choose arms without difference.

The shorter the weapons, the more dangerous, since those which can strike from close-by are of greater risk, as their blows cannot be easily parried due to the speed at which they arrive. In consequence, the partisan carries more danger than the spear, and the dagger more than the sword.

As two fencers fence, he who strikes with the riposte is more praiseworthy than he who strikes in first intention. This is because the former demonstrates how he toughens up after receiving the attack rather than losing heart.

After receiving a hit, you may not perform more than one riposte delivered with a single pass forward; concentrate all your thoughts to making good the one riposte, since it is with it that you will regain your honor.[54]

---

[52] Filippo Vadi gives the same advice from the other side of the equation: when you come to the half-sword, look for the opportunity to take the grip with your left hand.

[53] This and the following paragraph indicate how this form of swordsmanship is equally adapt for armored as well as unarmored play.

[54] Manciolino is citing a rule in the art of freeplay with the *spada da gioco*, which is also reported by the Anonymous Bolognese. The reasons given by the Anonymous are that such restriction makes the play more realistic (with sharp sword you may not physically be able to riposte with more than one pass after receiving a hit), and allow the spectator to have a clearer grasp of the action's outcome.

A blow to the head counts for three, because of the nobility of such part of the body. A blow to the foot counts for two, in deference to the awkwardness of delivering such a low attack.[55]

He who redoubles his attacks[56] is a valorous fencer.

Longer weapons are to be preferred to shorter ones: therefore, the spear is to be preferred to the *spiedo*, holding it against the latter not by the butt (dangerous because of the weapon's length) but at mid-haft and with good advantage. Similarly, it is better to take a partisan rather than a two-handed sword.

Delivering attacks from the waist up causes more danger in the opponent than doing so from the waist down, since the eyes (and consequently the heart) of the not-so-brave are easily conquered by such flashes.[57]

Be very mindful that the opponent does not have the slightest advantage of arms (or other factors), since this could cause you to lose.

Never disclose your offensive intentions to the opponent—rather, strive to guess the opponent's own tactics. This is because as you encounter each-other even-tempered you should make the most of all your designs. But if you fight for your honor, it is laudable to show your designs to the opponent.

---

[55] Apparent scoring conventions for school fencing; again showing the diversity of venues and applications with which the art was applied.

[56] In its simplest connotation, a redoubled attack is an offensive action in which more consecutive blows are delivered without interruption.

[57] Meaning that a sword swinging (i.e., flashing) towards the head and upper body of a timid fencer is more likely to conquer him by giving him more fear than one directed at his lower body. It was a common fencing adage in the Renaissance that attacks to the head and eyes tend to be more feared, especially by timid fencers.

OF COMBAT AND FENCING WITH ALL SORTS OF WEAPONS IN SIX BOOKS

Book One

For her security, our gallant art of arms bears with her ten defensive guards with twenty different names. I have considered it useful to speak of them here; for if they are learned forthwith, they will turn the rest of my book into a spacious, useful and well-lit field. Let me therefore begin my exposition with the help of God.

Chapter I: The Guards

THE GUARDIA ALTA

The first guard has the name of *Alta* (High). Set yourself elegantly upon your person, and hold the sword with the arm as high as possible. The sword will therefore point backwards. The buckler-hand should instead be well extended towards the opponent, stretching the arm as much as possible. Place your right foot about four fingers' width[58] in front of the left, the heel slightly raised. Keep both of your knees straight rather than bent.

This same guard can be formed in two additional ways. One is with the right foot in front of the left in a wide stance; the other is with the left foot forward in an equally wide stance. The sword and the buckler, however, should still be held as described above.

Therefore, as long as you hold the sword with the arm high in the air, the guard will always be called *Alta*, regardless of the position of your feet. The name of the guard depends in fact on the sword's position rather than that of the feet.

THE GUARDIA DI TESTA

The second guard is called *Guardia di Testa* (Head Guard). Form this by stretching the arms evenly towards the opponent, so that both fists are at shoulder-height. The only difference in the position of your hands is that the sword-hand should be slightly lower than the buckler-hand.

As for your feet, you can form this guard in two ways: right-foot forward or left-foot forward, both in a wide stance. Even in this case, the guard is still the same regardless of the placement of your feet, for the reason I mentioned above.

---

[58] This is approximately three inches.

THE GUARDIA DI FACCIA

The third guard is called *Guardia di Faccia* (Face Guard). It has two features in common with the Guardia di Testa and one difference. The commonalities are the positioning of the feet and the height of the arms. The difference is this: while in the Guardia di Testa your sword points sideways, in the Guardia di Faccia your sword is pointing straight to the opponent's face. Your buckler-hand should be placed right above your sword-hand.

THE GUARDIA DI SOPRA IL BRACCIO[59]

The fourth guard is called *Guardia di Sopra il Braccio* (Overarm Guard). Your sword-hand forms a cross by laying in the middle of your left arm, with the point of the sword facing backward. The buckler, instead, should be stretched toward the opponent.

A first way to position your feet in this guard is with the right just barely in front of the left, just enough that the two feet do not touch.

You can also form this same guard with the right foot forward in a wide stance, curving your body with the utmost grace. In this case, the position of the sword-hand should be the same, in the middle of the left arm. Otherwise, as I said, the guard would change its name. However, when the feet are thus positioned, your arms will be wider apart, whereas before they would have been tighter together. Your shoulder will thus face the opponent, so that you can attack him in whichever manner you please.

THE GUARDIA DI SOTTO IL BRACCIO

The fifth guard is called *Guardia di Sotto il Braccio* (Underarm Guard), because the sword-hand is located under the buckler-arm, just underneath the armpit, with the point of the sword facing backward. The buckler should be well extended towards the opponent.

As far as the feet, they can be situated as I described before: either with the right foot just barely in front of the left or with the right foot forward in a wide stance. In this last case, your right shoulder will be facing the opponent, as I also said about the fourth guard.

THE GUARDIA DI PORTA DI FERRO STRETTA

The sixth guard is called *Porta di Ferro Stretta* (Narrow Iron Gate). Position yourself sideways, so that your right shoulder—as described before—faces the opponent. Both arms should also be directed towards the opponent, but with the right arm extended downwards in defense of the right knee. Your sword-hand should be near and in the center of the right knee. The buckler-arm, on the other hand, should be extended straight towards the opponent, neither high nor low, so that it keeps the head well defended.

Place your right foot in front of the left in a wide stance, with the knee also facing the opponent. In this manner, the knee, a little curved, is defended by the sword-hand. The left foot should face sideways, with the left knee also bent.

---

[59] It is important to remark that *Sopra il Braccio* and *Sotto il Braccio* are also intended as positions where the sword swings to in relation to the left arm after performing a cut such as a full mandritto. Manciolino uses this reference several times (e.g., in the book on the plays or Assalti).

This guard is called *Porta di Ferro Stretta* by virtue of being safer than the others and of iron-like strength. Unlike in the *Porta di Ferro Larga*, which we will see next, in this guard the sword is held tightly close to the opponent while keeping an equally tight defense of the right knee.

THE GUARDIA PORTA DI FERRO LARGA

The seventh guard is called *Porta di Ferro Larga* (Wide Iron Gate). It originates from the previous guard, since the feet and the body move in the manner described above. The only difference is that the sword-hand is moved away from the knee: it should point towards the ground and be placed to the inside of the right knee.

The reason why it is called "wide"[60] is because the sword creates more of an opening than in the previous guard, as it pulls away from the knee.

THE CINGHIARA PORTA DI FERRO

The eighth guard is called *Cinghiara Porta di Ferro* (Wild Boar Iron Gate). Place your left foot[61] sideways with the knee slightly bent, and keep your right knee straight. Position your sword-hand before your left knee, in a way similar to the Porta di Ferro with which this guard shares part of its name. Place your left hand so that the buckler defends your head as I have described above.

This guard is called *Cinghiara* (wild boar) after the animal bearing that name, who, when attacked, sets himself with his head and tusks sideways in a similar offensive guard.

THE CODA LUNGA E ALTA

The ninth guard is called *Coda Lunga e Alta* (Long and High Tail). Place your left foot forward in a wide stance, with your knee slightly bent and the foot pointing straight at the opponent. Extend your right arm well towards the opponent, but with the well-gripped sword sideways so that it points straight at the opponent. The buckler-arm should be extended towards the opponent's face.

This guard and the next one originate from a guard called *Coda Lunga Alta*,[62] where the feet are placed in the same manner, but the sword and the arm are extended backward. It bears its name from the common proverb "do not embroil yourself with great masters, for they have a long tail," that is, they have the power to injure you by means of their numerous followers. So, that guard gave the name to this ninth and to the tenth, along with their great suitability to reach and strike the opponent.

Such is the guard named Coda Lunga e Alta.

---

[60] *Larga* is Italian for "wide."

[61] Although Manciolino does not specify it here, the left foot is forward of the right, as described by other authors such as Dall'Agocchie.

[62] It is likely that Manciolino means *Coda Lunga e Distesa*, "Long and Outstretched Tail," which is described and illustrated by Marozzo.

The Coda Lunga e Stretta

The tenth guard is called *Coda Lunga e Stretta* (Long and Narrow Tail). Place your right foot forward in a wide stance, in a way that the knee is slightly bent sideways.[63] Your arms should be positioned like in the Coda Lunga e Alta, save that the sword-arm should be slightly lower.

These guards will suffice for our purposes.

Chapter II: The Blows

Our valiant art is composed of two main virtues. Taking care of the defense right from the outset is the first; this is why the former chapter speaks about guards. The second is knowing how to attack your opponent in tempo without also getting hit. If you receive a hit while hitting your opponent, your glory would be naught, since this would make you simultaneously the victor and the vanquished. Do not, therefore, share your victory with the opponent, and do not let him share his shame with you.

But before I can teach you to hit, I need to reveal to you the names of the blows. There are five principal blows, and two secondary ones. The first is the mandritto; the second is the riverso; the third is the fendente; the fourth is the stoccata, or thrust. The fifth is the falso. The sword has two edges; the one towards the opponent is the true edge, while the one facing you is the false edge. So, if you deliver a natural cut to the opponent, directed from his left ear to his right knee (or any other part, as long as it originates from the opponent's left side), this is called a mandritto. If you deliver the opposite cut (that is, aimed at his right side—high or low), this is a riverso.[64]

If you lift the sword and place it in the middle of the two aforementioned cuts (that is, right to the top of the opponent's head and continuing downwards), this is the fendente. Conversely, every ascending cut you deliver towards either side of the opponent's face is the falso. Lastly, if you push a thrust against the opponent, this is universally called a stoccata (delivered with either foot forward, overhand or underhand).

Besides these five blows, there are two secondary ones; they are secondary because they are employed only in the art of sword and buckler. The first is the *stramazzone*; this is delivered from the wrist, making the sword turn down then up to the left of your sword-hand, and ending in a fendente-like cut. The other is the *montante*, and it is delivered upwards not unlike a falso ending in Guardia Alta.

Chapter III: The Attacks from Guardia Alta

Now that we have talked about the guards, the names of the blows and their delivery, we will move on to attacks, and then to how to defend against them. Since the best fencers are always poised in their guards to keep themselves safe, I will teach you how to unsettle and attack an opponent who stands in any of the ten guards we have seen; then, I will show you how he should defend against these attacks. We will start with the attacks from Guardia Alta.

---

[63] The sideways bend refers most likely to the left knee.

[64] Generic mandritti and riversi may be understood to be delivered like squalembrati, that is, proceeding obliquely downward.

If you and your opponent are in Guardia Alta, and you are the agent, you can:

1. Deliver a mandritto to his sword-hand ending Sopra il Braccio, come back with a riverso to the same target, and finish with a montante back into Guardia Alta. If you deliver these three blows, the opponent cannot attack you on any side without his hand meeting your blade.

2. Alternatively, you can deliver a riverso to his thigh; and if the opponent attacks your head, hit his sword-hand with a lateral falso going Sopra il Braccio.[65]

3. Feint a montante[66] while passing boldly forward with your left foot, ending in Guardia di Testa, where your sword will wait for the opponent's attack; right afterwards, pass with your right foot to his left, delivering a mandritto to his head in the same tempo; end with your left foot following behind the right[67] and set yourself in Guardia di Testa to remain safe.

4. Feint a riverso to his thigh while keeping your eyes on his sword-hand; if he attacks your head, deliver a mandritto (Sotto il Braccio) to his sword-hand, ensuring that the buckler defends your head, then retreat into safety with your right foot while delivering a riverso.

5. Deliver a stramazzone ending in Porta di Ferro Larga, so that he may attack you. Defend by going into Guardia di Testa while stepping forward with your right foot, and riposte with a mandritto to his face or leg, ensuring that your buckler guards your head. Then retreat into safety by passing back with your right foot while delivering a riverso.

6. Pass forward with your left foot and deliver a stramazzone to his right side; then, feint a riverso only to deliver a mandritto.

7. Feint a stramazzone and hit him with a mandritto.

8. Deliver an overhand thrust followed by one or two stramazzoni.

9. Attack him with a fendente accompanied by a stramazzone.

Here end the ways in which you can attack an opponent who stands in the aforementioned guard. If you were the one receiving the attack, following is a brief list of the counters (or ripostes).

---

[65] Meaning a falso directed right to left (rather than ascending), and ending Sopra il Braccio.

[66] Generally, ascending cuts delivered from Guardia Alta are prepared by swinging the sword backwards, then back up in front.

[67] This is a compass step (see the Primer of Bolognese Swordsmanship).

Chapter IV: The Counters to the Attacks from Guardia Alta

No matter which of the attacks the opponent chooses while you are in Guardia Alta, hit the rim of your buckler with your sword three or four times up and down, using the fendente and the falso. By doing this, you will be most safe against any offense.[68]

Against any of the attacks, you could also pull your right foot wide behind the left foot while delivering a montante-like thrust ending in Guardia di Faccia.

Chapter V: The Attacks from Guardia di Testa

If you are both situated in this guard and you want to attack, you can:

1. Deliver a mandritto to his face, flank or leg.

2. Push a thrust to his face and deliver a stramazzone.

3. Feint a mandritto and deliver a riverso.

4. Deliver two mandritti.

5. Feint a stramazzone and deliver a mandritto.

Chapter VI: The Counters to the Attacks from Guardia di Testa

Here are the counters to the attacks listed above:

1. Against the mandritto to the flank, the leg or the face, pull your right foot wide behind the left foot and void the mandritto; then, from Coda Lunga e Alta push a thrust to his face while passing forward with your right foot into a wide stance and delivering a mandritto to his face in the same tempo.

2. Against the thrust and stramazzone, parry the thrust with your sword. And when he turns the stramazzoni,[69] place your sword-hand under your buckler, aiming the point to his hand.

3. Against the mandritto, place your sword into Guardia di Faccia. And against the riverso (high or low), parry with the sword and immediately deliver a mandritto in any way you want.

4. Against the two mandritti, cut a half mandritto to his sword-hand and into the rim of your buckler, setting yourself into Porta di Ferro Stretta; as he delivers the second mandritto, parry it with a falso and come down with a mandritto to his face, while stepping forward with your right foot to better reach him.

5. If he feinted a stramazzone to deliver a mandritto, stop the feint with a mandritto, ending with your sword in Porta di Ferro Stretta; when the opponent delivers the mandritto, hit into it with a falso and finish with a riverso to his thigh.

---

[68] Most likely, Manciolino advocates hitting the right side of the buckler's rim (from your perspective). Hitting the rim of the buckler while executing this defensive action ensures two things: firstly, you keep your weapons joined; secondly, you do not risk making your motions too large.

[69] Plural here, while in the previous sentence and in the attacks sections it was singular.

Chapter VII: The Attacks from Guardia di Faccia

If you are both in guard, and you are to attack, you can:

1. Push a thrust to the opponent's face.

2. Provoke the opponent with a strong mandritto.

3. Or with a stramazzone.

4. Or (if you prefer) hit a falso to his sword and deliver a cut to his face.

5. Feint an ascending riverso and deliver a mandritto.

Chapter VIII: The Counters to the Attacks from Guardia di Faccia

Please know that:

1. If the opponent pushes a thrust, pass with the left foot towards his right side, while performing a mezza volta with your sword-hand; this will leave the opponent to your outside. Then, strike him in the face.

2. As he lifts his sword-hand to deliver a mandritto, present your point to him, which will give him enough fear to interrupt his action.

3. If he delivers a stramazzone, you can parry with a falso, turning your false edge towards his left side; this will not only parry his stramazzone, but it will cause your edge to hit his face as well.

4. If he hits a falso to your sword to cut to your face, quickly perform a mezza volta with your sword-hand, which will keep you safe.

5. If he feints an ascending riverso to deliver a mandritto, pull your right foot in a wide stance behind the left while pushing your true edge against his sword-hand.

Chapter IX: The Attacks from Guardia di Sopra il Braccio

I will say this here once and for all: the attacks I describe in these chapters are supposed to be effected between two opponents standing in the same guard.

1. Deliver a riverso.

2. Feint two riversi, and attack with a mandritto.

3. Cut a riverso into your buckler-rim.

4. Feint a riverso and deliver a mandritto.

5. Pass with your left foot towards the opponent's right side, feinting a riverso; then, pass with your right foot towards his left side and deliver a fendente to his head. Lastly, let your left leg follow behind the right.

6. Feint a punta riversa from Sopra il Braccio and deliver a stramazzone.

7. Deliver a riverso, a fendente and a stramazzone at the same time.

8. Pass forward with your left foot and push a thrust over the buckler; then, pass with the right foot and deliver either a mandritto or a stramazzone as you prefer.

9. [Deliver two stramazzoni.][70]

10. Push your right foot towards the opponent's right side, delivering a *riverso spinto*[71] or a mandritto.

Chapter X: The Counters to the Attacks from Guardia di Sopra il Braccio

1. [At the riverso: Manciolino does not supply a counter.]

2. At the two riversi: parry the first one with the sword; when the second arrives, gather your right foot near the left and then pass forward with the left foot delivering a *riverso spinto* to the opponent's face. If he were only feinting the two riversi to attack you with a mandritto, pass backward with your right foot, going into Cinghiara Porta di Ferro. As soon as he delivers the mandritto, pass again forward with your right foot, hitting into his cut with the false edge of your sword and delivering a riverso.

3. At the riverso into the buckler-rim: turn a mandritto to his face.

4. At his feinting the riverso to attack you with a mandritto: protect yourself against the feint by going into Guardia di Faccia. When he delivers the mandritto, make yourself small under your sword, parrying the blow; then, quickly pass with your left foot towards his right side, pushing a riverso into his right temple. Then let your right leg follow behind the left.

5. At his passing with his left foot and feinting a riverso: set yourself in Guardia di Faccia. When he passes towards your left side to attack you with a fendente, deliver a sideways riverso to his temple.

6. At the punta riversa: parry with the sword. As he delivers the two stramazzoni,[72] set your sword into Guardia di Testa and parry them, answering with a mandritto to your opponent's face.

---

[70] In some instances, such as this, Manciolino does not match exactly the attacks with the counters. These two stramazzoni, for example, are not mentioned as an attack, but appear in the next chapter on counters.

[71] Literally: a "pushed riverso." This is a cut where the slicing element is accomplished by pushing rather than pulling. A "push-cut."

[72] This is inconsistent with point 6 of the previous chapter, where the punta riversa feint was only followed by a single stramazzone.

7. At the riverso: turn your sword-point towards his hand, joined with the buckler. At the fendente, parry by going with your sword into Guardia di Testa. At the stramazzone, pass forward with your left foot in a wide stance, parry his blow with the buckler and attack with a stoccata to his flank. Then, retreat with a backward jump.

8. At his passing with his left foot and attacking you in the face with a thrust Sopra il Braccio: parry with the sword. As he passes with his right foot and attacks you with the mandritto: in the moment when his blow has not yet fallen, give him a riverso to his right thigh.

9. At the two stramazzoni: parry them with your right foot forward and your sword in Guardia di Testa; then, push a thrust into the opponent's face.

10. At his passing with his left foot towards your right side to attack your face with the riverso spinto: turn a falso to his right temple, leaving your buckler to the defense of your head. If he delivers the mandritto, gather your right foot near the left, lifting your sword-arm high and voiding the blow. Then, push forward with your right foot and answer him with a mandritto to the head.

Chapter XI: The Attacks from Guardia di Sotto il Braccio

1. Attack with a riverso to the face.

2. Deliver a falso followed by a mandritto to the face.

3. Deliver a riverso while pulling back with your left foot.

4. Push a thrust into the opponent's hand.

5. With your left foot forward, raise a falso and in the same tempo, push a montante-like thrust, passing forward with your right foot and delivering a stramazzone, ending in Porta di Ferro Stretta.

Chapter XII: The Counters to the Attacks from Guardia di Sotto il Braccio

1. At the riverso to the face: pass with your left foot towards the opponent's right side and in that tempo deliver a riverso to his right temple.

2. At the falso followed by a mandritto: lift the false edge of your sword and, as he throws the mandritto, pass back with your right foot in a wide stance, cut a half mandritto into his sword, ending in Cinghiara Porta di Ferro. Then, immediately pass forward with your right foot in a wide stance, pushing a thrust to the opponent's face followed by a mandritto to his shins.

3. At the riverso while pulling back: pass forward with your left foot, at the same time delivering a riverso to the opponent's face.

4. At the thrust to your sword-hand: pass backward with your right foot in a wide stance and set your sword in Coda Lunga e Alta.

5. At the falso going into Guardia Alta: set yourself in that same guard. As he attacks you with the montante-like thrust, pull your right foot behind the left, going into Cinghiara Porta di Ferro. When he attacks you with the stramazzone, pass again forward with your right foot in a wide stance, parry with a falso and deliver a mandritto to his face.

Chapter XIII: The Attacks from Porta di Ferro Stretta

1. Deliver a stramazzone.

2. Pass forward with your left foot, pushing a thrust to the opponent's face; then, pass forward with the right foot, delivering two stramazzoni.

3. Feint a stramazzone and deliver a riverso to the opponent's thigh.

4. Push a thrust to the opponent's face and, passing forward with the left foot, feint a riverso to his head and deliver instead a mandritto to the head or leg, as you prefer.

5. Push a thrust with a left-foot pass, then pass forward with your right foot in a wide stance, delivering an ascending riverso to his arms; then, immediately cut a mandritto to his head or leg. For your defense, throw a riverso to your opponent's sword-hand, pulling your right foot in a wide stance behind the left; this is also a good way to thwart the last two blows.

Chapter XIV: The Counters to the Attacks from Porta di Ferro Stretta

1. At the stramazzone: as his hand starts to turn, turn your own false edge towards his left side, thereby protecting yourself from the cut. Then, attack his face with your true edge.

2. At his passing with his left foot and attacking you with a thrust to the face: hit into the thrust and raise your sword into Guardia di Faccia. As he delivers the stramazzone, make yourself small under your sword in Guardia di Faccia and parry the cut with your true edge. Then, immediately pass forward and to his right with your left foot in a wide stance, and deliver a riverso to his right temple. End by letting your right leg follow behind the left.

3. If he feints a stramazzone, get into Guardia di Faccia, and as he delivers the riverso to your thigh, immediately throw your right leg behind the left while hitting his sword-arm with a riverso.

4. As he pushes a thrust with his left foot forward to hit you in the face, parry with the false edge; when he feints the riverso, perform a mezza volta with your sword-hand, and as he delivers the mandritto, hit a half mandritto to his sword-hand.

5. If he pushes a thrust with the left foot forward to hit you in the face, throw your right foot obliquely behind your left foot, getting into Cinghiara Porta di Ferro; and if he passes forward with his right foot feinting a riverso to deliver a mandritto to your head, parry the mandritto with the false edge, pass forward with your right foot and riposte with a mandritto to his face.

Chapter XV: The Attacks from Porta di Ferro Larga

You can:

1. Perform a falso and riverso.

2. Lift a falso and deliver a mandritto to his face, performing a gathering step forward (right foot forward).

3. Deliver two thrusts; one straight to his face, while passing with your left foot towards his right side; the other (afterwards) by withdrawing your hand,[73] then pushing the point into his flank while passing with your right foot towards his left side. And in order to deliver this thrust with fewer impediments, you can place your buckler against his blade and let your left foot follow behind the right. After this, hit his head with a fendente.

4. Step forward with your right foot and deliver a riverso to his head.

5. Or lift a falso up to Guardia di Faccia followed by a stramazzone.

6. Deliver a falso into Guardia Alta.

7. Deliver a drilled thrust[74] followed by a stramazzone.

Chapter XVI: The Counters to Attacks from Porta di Ferro Larga

1. When the opponent delivers a falso and riverso, hit his falso with one of your own, and to defend against the riverso, turn a mandritto to his left temple.

2. As he lifts the falso and delivers the mandritto, feint a falso, but withdraw your sword-hand and push a thrust to his face while he attacks you with the mandritto. Then, quickly pass with your left foot towards his right side, delivering a riverso to his head.

---

[73] In the 17th century, withdrawing the arm in preparation for a thrust fell out of favor, as tempi became shorter in predominantly-thrusting fencing styles. However, this was rather the norm in Manciolino's time. This is especially the case when multiple thrusts are delivered.

[74] A drilled thrust (*punta trivellata*) is occasionally found but not satisfactorily defined in extant swordsmanship treatises. Going by its name, it may be a thrust delivered while performing a mezza volta with the sword-hand, thus making the blade turn, drill-like as the point makes contact with the target. This, however, is simply an educated guess.

3. If he delivers the two thrusts, parry the first one with your false edge. While he steps forward with his right foot to deliver the second, parry with your true edge, then parry his fendente to the head by going in Guardia di Faccia, riposting with a riverso to his thigh.

4. If he passes with his left foot towards his right side to attack your face with a falso, parry with the false edge.

5. As he passes with his right foot to deliver a riverso, parry in Guardia di Testa, and riposte with a mandritto to the face or leg (as you prefer). If he turns stramazzoni, get into Guardia di Faccia and you will be safe.[75]

6. As he delivers the falso into Guardia Alta, void his cut.

7. When he delivers the thrust, parry it with the false edge. If he attacks with a stramazzone, pass with the left foot towards his right side and hit his sword-arm with a stramazzone, letting your right foot follow behind the left.

Chapter XVII: The Attacks from Cinghiara Porta di Ferro

As you are in Cinghiara Porta di Ferro, you can:

1. Push a thrust to the opponent's face with a right-foot pass, followed by a mandritto (against an opponent who is in the same guard) or by a riverso to the leg.

2. [Push a thrust and deliver a riverso to his face.][76]

3. After the thrust, you can pass with the left foot towards his right side, place the buckler under his sword-hand and deliver a mandritto to his leg, letting your right foot follow behind the left.

4. Push two thrusts; the first with a right-foot pass, the second by quickly passing with your left foot towards his right side, drawing your sword-hand towards you and pushing the thrust to his face.

5. Raise a falso into Guardia di Faccia while passing forward with your right foot, then strike him with a mandritto.

6. Push a thrust followed by a stramazzone, also with a right-foot pass.

7. Push the same thrust, feint a riverso and strike him with a mandritto.

8. Push the thrust, then withdraw the hand and follow with a drilled thrust.

---

[75] The order of counters 4 and 5 is inverted from the list of attacks.

[76] This attack is not mentioned here, but it appears in the next chapter where it is countered.

Chapter XVIII: The Counters to the Attacks from Cinghiara Porta di Ferro

1. As the opponent pushes a thrust with his right foot forward, parry with the false edge; against the mandritto, throw your left foot behind the right and deliver a half mandritto to his sword-arm.

2. As he pushes the thrust, parry with the false edge; as you see the riverso coming against your face, pass forward with your right foot and parry in Guardia di Testa and riposte with a mandritto to his face.

3. When he delivers the thrust with his right foot forward, parry with the false edge; as he passes forward with the left foot to strike you across the leg with a mandritto, throw your right foot behind the left and hit his hand with a half mandritto.

4. If he pushes two thrusts, pass forward with your right foot and parry the first one with the false edge; parry the second one with the true edge while passing forward with the left foot, and deliver a falso to his face.

5. If he raises a falso to strike you with a mandritto with the right foot forward, throw your left foot behind your right and get into Porta di Ferro Larga; as he starts the mandritto to your head, parry it with the false edge and strike a mandritto to his face.

6. If he pushes a thrust with his right foot forward, followed by a stramazzone, parry the thrust with the false edge and the stramazzone by going into Guardia di Faccia.

7. If he pushes the thrust with his right foot forward, parry with the false edge without any footwork; as he feints the riverso, pass forward with your right foot and turn your true edge against his feint. Then, parry his mandritto to your head by going into Guardia di Testa, riposting with a similar cut to his face.

8. If he pushes a thrust with his right foot forward, cut a stramazzone to his sword without moving your feet; and as he delivers the drilled thrust, pass forward with your right foot into a wide stance, parry with the false edge and push a really good one to his face.[77]

Chapter XIX: The Attacks from Coda Lunga e Alta (Left Foot Forward)

1. Pass forward with your right foot while cutting falso and mandritto.

2. Pass forward with the right foot and cut the falso, then feint a mandritto and deliver a riverso.

---

[77] The implied word for "a really good one" is "thrust," in this colorful colloquialism by Manciolino.

3. After passing forward with the aforementioned foot, push a thrust and deliver a mandritto.

4. Pass with the right foot, deliver a thrust followed by a riverso.[78]

5. Pull the left foot next to the right, pass forward with the right foot and deliver a fendente.

6. Push a thrust accompanied by a stramazzone, with a right-foot pass.

7. Push a thrust to his face with a right-foot pass, then pass with the left foot towards his right side, place the buckler under his sword and deliver a mandritto to his leg, letting your left foot follow behind the right.[79]

Chapter XX: The Counters to Attacks from Coda Lunga e Alta

1. As the opponent passes forward with his right foot and strikes falso and mandritto, set yourself into Cinghiara Porta di Ferro (without moving your feet). While he delivers the mandritto, pass forward with your right foot, hitting his mandritto with your false edge and immediately delivering a mandritto to his face or leg (as you prefer).

2. If he does the falso, then feints a mandritto, pass forward with your right foot and get into Guardia di Faccia; as he turns the riverso to your thigh, pass forward with your left foot, turn your point towards the ground and parry; then, immediately push a thrust to his face.

3. If he delivers a thrust with the right foot forward to deliver a mandritto, counter the thrust by passing forward with your right foot and parrying with your true edge; against the mandritto, push a thrust to his face without moving your feet.

4. If he passes forward with his right foot to deliver a thrust and a riverso, thwart the thrust by also passing forward with your right foot and parrying with the true edge; against the riverso to your leg, throw your right foot behind your left[80] hitting his sword-arm with a riverso of your own.

5. If he performed a changing step to attack you with a fendente, repair into Porta di Ferro; and as he passes forward with his right foot to give you the fendente, set yourself into Guardia di Testa and parry, then deliver a mandritto to the face or leg (as you prefer).

---

[78] In the counter section, Manciolino speaks of the riverso being to the leg.

[79] Here, Manciolino either omits an additional pass or mistakenly switches feet (I believe the latter to be more likely).

[80] Manciolino states "throw your right foot behind your right," which is likely a typographical error or a mistake.

6. If he pushes a thrust with the aforementioned foot forward to attack you with a stramazzone, parry it[81] by hitting it with a falso; pass with your right foot towards his left side, deliver a mandritto to his head and let your left foot follow behind your right.

7. If he pushes a thrust with his right foot forward, then passes with his left foot to deliver a mandritto to your leg, parry the thrust with a falso. As he passes to deliver the mandritto, throw your left foot back and cut a mandritto to his sword-hand.

Chapter XXI: The Attacks from Coda Lunga e Stretta (Right Foot Forward)

1. Push a thrust with a left-foot pass, then pass with the right foot and deliver a mandritto.

2. Push the same thrust, then pass with the right foot and turn a stramazzone.

3. Push the same thrust, then pass with the right foot, feint a mandritto and deliver a riverso to his face or leg.

4. Push the same thrust, then pass with your right foot and deliver a fendente to his head.

Chapter XXII: The Counters to the Attacks from Coda Lunga e Stretta (Right Foot Forward)

1. As he pushes the thrust with his left foot forward to strike you with a mandritto, parry the thrust with a falso; against the mandritto, do not move your feet and cut a half mandritto into his sword-hand.

2. If, after the same thrust, he attacks with a stramazzone, parry the thrust with your true edge, and defend against the stramazzone by going into Guardia di Faccia and with no footwork.

3. If, after the thrust, he feinted a mandritto to attack you with a riverso, defend against the thrust by pushing a similar one against him, so that the swords will meet with their true edges; against the mandritto, go into Guardia di Faccia without any other motion. If the riverso is to your face, perform a mezza volta with your hand and hit into the incoming cut, following with a mandritto to his leg or face. If the riverso is to your leg, go forward with your left foot towards his right side and push a thrust to his face, letting your right foot follow behind your left.

---

[81] Manciolino says *quello* (masculine for "it"); since *punta* (thrust) is feminine and *stramazzone* is masculine, "it" likely refers to the stramazzone.

4. If, after the thrust, he attacks your head with a fendente, parry the thrust with a half mandritto to his sword-hand; against the fendente, get quickly into Guardia di Testa, and thus protected, riposte with a mandritto to his face or leg (as you prefer).

Book Two

Having suitably described the ten famed guards as well as the offenses they may spawn in the previous book, in this second book I will diligently offer instruction in three masterful plays (or assalti) with the sword and small buckler. These will be well-received by students, as they help make the body, the legs and the hands lively and quick. Therefore, he who does not take delight in stepping in tempo and in the way I will teach (and have taught), will enjoy neither grace nor victory in his fencing.

Not grace, for just as rich fabrics adorn the charming and lovely Nymphs lightly treading on Mount Menalus or in the Lyceum, so does supple stepping embellish the blows of the dazzling sword. Were our weapon despoiled of its proper steps, it would fall into the darkness of a serene night being orphaned of the stars. And how can white-clad Victory be, where gentle grace is lacking?

We shan't therefore call him victor who wins by chance and throws random blows like a brutal peasant; nor shall we call vanquished him who proceeds according to the correct teachings. It is indeed more respected among knowledgeable men to lose with poise than to win erratically and outside of any elegance.

The hand of fortune is sometimes found in vile disgrace; but Victory always sits upon a grace that is never tyrannical. I therefore conclude that never will loss visit the polished fencer, even after he perchance receives a hit.

Before commencing our task, I will teach how to enter the play, so that good fencers may not only be skilled in the offense and the defense, but may also embellish their actions through graceful motions of the body.

The First Assalto

Firstly, you will set yourself against your opponent on one side of the salle (or other large space), nimbly standing over your feet. Hold the sword and the buckler so that every movement, every action and every gesture may be full of grace. As you start approaching the opponent, you will:

1. Pass with the right foot obliquely towards your right side, while delivering a falso against the boss of your buckler and going into Guardia Alta, with the buckler held in front of your face like a mirror.

2. Pass forward with the left foot and perform a *ritocco* of the buckler,[82] placing your sword in Guardia di Testa and lowering your buckler alongside your left thigh.

3. Pass forward with the right foot and lift your sword into Guardia Alta.

4. Pass forward with the left foot, executing a montante accompanied by a mandritto Sopra il Braccio, and getting into Guardia di Testa.

---

[82] As it appears in Marozzo, this is likely an action in which you give a pommel-strike to the inside of the face of your own buckler.

5. Pass forward with your right foot, hit the boss of your buckler with a falso and execute a montante up to Guardia Alta.

6. Then, you have the embellishment:

   a. Throw your right foot behind the left while cutting a fendente into the rim of the buckler; let the sword continue downward and behind you all the way up into Guardia Alta.

   b. Pull your left foot behind the right and perform a *ritocco* of the buckler.

   c. Pass forward with your left foot into a wide stance, getting into Guardia di Testa.

   d. Pass forward with your right foot hitting a falso into the boss of your buckler.

   e. Lift a montante into Guardia Alta pulling your right foot next to the left, and making sure that your buckler keeps your head well defended.

Up to here, I have described the way to come and meet your opponent. Dear reader, please do not forget the embellishment, since I will reuse it at different points in this assalto without describing it again.

But now you are close to the opponent, so it is no longer time to throw blows into the wind.

1. Pass forward with your right foot into a wide stance, delivering a mandritto to the opponent's face that goes into Sopra il Braccio, and come back with a riverso lowering your sword into Coda Lunga e Stretta, making sure that your buckler keeps your head well defended.

2. Pull your right foot near your left, quickly raising a montante to Guardia Alta.

3. Pass forward with your right foot, delivering a fendente into Guardia di Faccia.

4. Pass with the left foot towards the opponent's right side, delivering a stramazzone into Cinghiara Porta di Ferro, guarding your head with your buckler.

5. Pass forward with the right foot into a wide stance, deliver a sideways falso to the opponent's face, so that afterwards the sword lifts into Guardia Alta.

6. Pull your right foot near the left and deliver a mandritto to the head or face, that goes Sopra il Braccio.

7. Pass forward again with your right foot into a wide stance, throwing your sword-hand upwards and delivering a mandritto to the opponent's face, that goes Sotto il Braccio.

8. Pull the right foot next to the left, defending with your buckler.

9. Pass forward with your right foot, delivering a falso up to Guardia di Faccia, followed by two stramazzoni the last of which puts you into Porta di Ferro Stretta.

10. And from here, pull the right foot next to the left, cutting a montante up to Guardia Alta.

Then, perform the embellishment as you have been taught.

11. Pass forward with your right foot, delivering a mandritto Sopra il Braccio and pulling your right foot back near the left.

12. Pass forward with your right foot and deliver two riversi: the first to the opponent's face, the other to his thigh.

13. While withdrawing your right foot near the left, deliver an overhand thrust that goes Sopra il Braccio.

14. Pass forward with the left foot while pushing a punta riversa into his face.

15. Pass forward with the right foot into a wide stance, delivering an ascending riverso, quickly turn a falso to his left temple and give a pushed riverso to the right side of his face.

16. Immediately throw the right foot behind the left in a wide stance, delivering a mandritto that goes into Guardia di Faccia, followed by a mezza volta getting you into Coda Lunga e Alta; keep your head well protected by the buckler.

17. Pull the left foot back near the right, then pass forward with the right foot pushing a thrust to the opponent's face accompanied by a riverso to the thigh, finishing into Coda Lunga e Stretta.

18. Pass forward with your left foot, pushing a thrust to his face.

19. Pass forward with your right foot, delivering a stramazzone to his head that ends in Porta di Ferro Stretta, keeping your head well protected by the buckler.

20. Pull your right foot near the left and perform a montante up to Guardia Alta.

21. Then, perform the embellishment as you have been taught.

22. Pass forward with your right foot and deliver a mandritto Sopra il Braccio; then, immediately pull your right foot back near the left.

23. Pass forward with your right foot, delivering a punta riversa to the opponent's face.

24. Pass with the left foot towards his right side, turning a stramazzone to his face.

25. Pass forward with your right foot and turn a stramazzone to the opponent's face, followed by a thrust into Guardia di Faccia accompanied by your buckler.

26. Turn a third stramazzone to the opponent's head, down to Porta di Ferro Stretta, and pull your right foot back near the left while lifting a montante into Guardia Alta.

Then perform the embellishment as you have been taught.

27. Perform a *stretta* of the half-sword,[83] by passing forward with your right foot in a wide stance, delivering a mandritto Sotto il Braccio and pulling your right foot back next to the left.

---

[83] This is an action of the *strette* of the half sword, also called narrow play. For an explanation of this concept, please refer to the technical introduction (primer) to the Bolognese style.

28. Again, pass forward with your right foot in a wide stance, delivering a sideways falso into Guardia di Faccia.

29. Pass forward with your left foot and execute a mezza volta with your sword-hand, accompanied by a thrust to the opponent's face.

30. Pass with your right foot towards the opponent's left side while feinting a mandritto to his left side; in the same tempo, pull your right foot back and push a riverso into his right temple.

31. Pull your left foot back and strike the opponent with a half mandritto into Guardia di Faccia.

Then, place your right foot near your left, get into Guardia Alta and execute the embellishment as you have been taught.

After giving you the play you would use against the opponent, I will offer you a retreat from play, which is no less dazzling than the entry into the play that I have described at the beginning of the assalto.

1. Pull your right foot back behind the left, and deliver a mandritto Sotto il Braccio.

2. Pass back with your left foot executing a montante to your left side, so that the sword goes up in Guardia Alta.

3. Pull your right foot back near the left executing another montante to your right side, and going up again in Guardia Alta.

4. Step back with your right foot while delivering a mandritto Sotto il Braccio.

5. Perform a mezza volta with your body towards your right, while your sword gets out from under your arm and turns above your head into Guardia di Alicorno, meaning that your sword-hand is high and your point directed downwards.[84]

6. Then, throw your left foot behind the right in a wide stance, pushing an ascending thrust going up into Guardia Alta.

7. End by pulling your right foot next to the left, which will place you where you had begun.

---

[84] This means: from the Guardia di Sotto il Braccio, forcefully turn your body to your right while delivering an ascending, left-to-right cut that brings the sword and the sword-hand high above your head; then, let the sword turn clockwise above your head until the point is forward and slightly sloping down, the hand still high (the Guardia di Alicorno). Manciolino does not describe edge-orientation, so a variety of options may be equally possible.

The Second Assalto

It should be already clear by reading the first one that assalti are divided into three parts. The first is the entry into the play; the second is the play; the third is the retreat from the play. While the second part has offensive blows, the blows of the first and third parts are "blanks" and flourishes. Let us begin the second assalto with the first part, which is the entry into the play.

Set yourself in a corner of the salle as you did before, in the first graceful posture. Then:

1. Pass towards your right with your right foot, striking a falso into the boss of your buckler, lifting the sword into Guardia Alta and placing the buckler in front of your face, turned towards you as if it were a mirror.

2. Pass forward with your left foot in a wide stance, leap sprightly towards the opponent, in which tempo the sword executes a stramazzone into Porta di Ferro Stretta, which will let you end even-footed.

3. Pass forward with the right foot in a wide stance, executing a montante into Guardia Alta.

4. Perform an embellishment, which is different than the one in the first assalto (the embellishments, as I like to call them, are different for each assalto; you can use for the whole play the one that is at the beginning of each):

    a. Begin the embellishment of the second assalto by cutting a fendente into the rim of the buckler, down to Cinghiara Porta di Ferro while passing back with your right foot.

    b. Pass with the left foot behind the right, and hit the boss of the buckler.[85]

    c. Pull the right foot next to the left and execute a montante into Guardia Alta.

Now, to attack the opponent, you will do the following:

1. Pass forward with your left foot in a wide stance, delivering a montante-like thrust to his face.

2. Pass forward with your right foot also in a wide stance, delivering a drilled riverso[86] to his face, redoubled by two stramazzoni to the head with the last one ending in Porta di Ferro Stretta.

3. Perform a montante into Guardia Alta while pulling your right foot near the left.

---

[85] Manciolino does not specify with what part of the sword; the false edge would be a stylistically-viable choice.

[86] *Riverso trivellato.* This, like the drilled thrust, is never defined in swordsmanship treatises extant as of this writing; however, we can infer it is a pushed riverso incorporating a mezza volta at the time the point arrives on target, causing the sword-blade to turn like a drill.

4. Pass forward with the right foot and deliver a mandritto Sopra il Braccio, then recover your right foot near the left.

5. Pass forward with your left foot and deliver a half riverso ending in Guardia di Faccia.

6. Pass forward with your right foot, feinting another riverso, then feinting a mandritto to the head.[87]

7. Pass forward with your left foot and deliver a montante-like thrust to his face.

8. Pass forward with your right foot and deliver an ascending riverso, followed by a mandritto going Sopra il Braccio.

9. Throw your right foot behind the left, delivering a riverso to the opponent's sword-hand and ensuring that your head is well defended by the buckler; end in Coda Lunga.

10. With your left foot forward, bring your sword into Guardia di Testa.

11. Pass with your right foot to the opponent's left side, delivering a fendente to his head, while your left foot follows behind the right and your sword gets into Porta di Ferro Stretta, then into Guardia di Faccia.

12. Pass with your left foot towards his left side, delivering a riverso to his face and letting your right foot follow behind the left.

13. After this, retreat backward with a sprightly jump[88] and, passing forward with your right foot, deliver a montante into Guardia Alta.

14. Pull your right foot near the left.

Perform the embellishment as you have been taught.

15. Resuming the play with your right foot forward, deliver a fendente going into Guardia di Faccia while pulling your right foot near the left.

16. Stepping forward with your left foot, deliver a stramazzone to his head.

17. Following with a right-foot forward pass, feint a stramazzone, but strike his forward leg with a mandritto, with your sword going Sotto Braccio; keep the head well defended by the buckler.

18. Deliver an ascending riverso to the opponent's sword-hand while immediately retreating with a sprightly jump, in such a way that after jumping you will be even-footed in Coda Lunga e Alta.[89]

---

[87] Here is an instance of a double feint in the Bolognese style.

[88] Given the footwork before and after, this jump should be performed without altering the relationship between the feet.

[89] Given the footwork before and after, this jump should be performed in conjunction with a backward pass with the right foot.

19. Pass forward with your right foot and deliver a montante up to Guardia Alta.

20. Deliver a stramazzone down to Porta di Ferro Larga, leaving yourself open for an attack.

21. If the opponent attacks your head, throw your left foot forward, set your sword in Coda Lunga and parry his attack with your buckler; riposte with a sideways falso to the right temple, letting your sword go Sotto il Braccio.

22. Throw your left foot behind the right, delivering a riverso to his face that goes into Coda Lunga, letting your head be well defended by the buckler.

23. Pull your right foot back, pushing a thrust to his face.

24. Go again forward with your right foot and redouble two stramazzoni against him, so that the last one ends in Porta di Ferro Stretta, followed by a montante ending in Guardia Alta.

Perform the embellishment as you have been taught.

25. Pass forward with your right foot and deliver a stramazzone, ending in Porta di Ferro Larga, ensuring that your head is well defended by the buckler.

26. Gather forward with your left foot and deliver a falso, ending in Guardia di Faccia.

27. Step forward with your right foot and deliver a sideways mandritto to his face, resetting your sword in Porta di Ferro.

28. Get into Guardia di Testa, attack the opponent's leg with a mandritto going Sotto il Braccio.

29. Gather back with your right foot and strike his sword-hand with a riverso, ending with your sword in Coda Lunga.

30. Step forward with your right foot and push a thrust to his face.

31. As he lifts his sword to parry, place your buckler immediately under his sword, pass with your left foot towards his right side and deliver a mandritto to his leg; let your right foot follow behind the left.

32. Pull your left foot behind the right in a wide stance, performing a mezza volta with your hand so that you end in Coda Lunga e Stretta.

33. Push a thrust to his face without any footwork.

34. Pass with your left foot towards his right side, delivering a riverso to his right temple; then let your right foot follow behind the left, while ensuring that your head is well defended by the buckler.

35. Push a thrust to the opponent's face, retreat with a brisk jump and set yourself in Coda Lunga e Alta.[90]

---

[90] Given the footwork before and after, this jump should be performed without altering the relationship between the feet.

36. Pass forward with your right foot and push a thrust to his face, feint a mandritto to his head and strike him instead with a riverso to his right temple, with your sword ending in Coda Lunga.

37. Deliver a sideways falso to his sword-hand (going Sopra il Braccio), lift your sword-hand in the air and deliver a mandritto to his face that goes Sotto il Braccio.

38. Pull your right foot back and attack his sword-hand with a riverso.

39. Pass forward with your right foot, push a thrust to his face, feint a riverso to the face, attacking him instead with a sideways mandritto to his right temple, ending with your sword in Porta di Ferro Stretta; ensure that your head is well guarded by the buckler.

40. Pull your right foot back and perform a mezza volta with your hand, ending in Coda Lunga e Stretta.

41. Without any footwork, cut a half mandritto to his sword-hand, ending in Cinghiara Porta di Ferro.

42. Pass forward with your right foot and push a thrust to his face, redoubling two stramazzoni to his head (and keeping your head protected by the buckler).

43. Pull your right foot back near the left and lift a montante up to Guardia Alta.

Embellish the play as you have been taught.

44. Perform a stretta of the half sword by delivering a stramazzone ending in Porta di Ferro Larga, then stepping forward with your left foot pushing a thrust to his face on his right side; as he lifts his sword to parry, grab his sword from the inside with your left hand and deliver a mandritto to his head (or wherever you want); this will satisfactorily end the play.

To perform a graceful return from play:

1. Going backward, pass back with your right foot while delivering a mandritto going Sotto il Braccio.

2. Pass back with your left foot and deliver a montante to your left side, then one on your right, ending in Guardia Alta.

3. Pass again back with your right foot and deliver a mandritto, going Sotto il Braccio.

4. Then, turn your body to your right over your stationary feet, deliver a riverso and make sure that your sword turns above your head and ends in Guardia di Alicorno (just as you did the other time).[91]

---

[91] See the footnote in the return of play from the First Assalto.

5. Throw your left foot back, pushing a thrust into Guardia Alta

6. Pull your right foot near the right, ending where you started the entry into the play.

The Third Assalto

Not unlike you did in the previous two assalti, set yourself with the utmost elegance in a corner of the salle. As you prepare to fence your opponent:

1. Pass obliquely with your right foot to your right, executing a *mulinetto* (that is, a rotating turn of the sword to the outside of the sword-arm).

2. Pass forward with your left foot, cutting an ascending riverso into Sopra il Braccio.

3. Pass forward with your right foot and deliver two riversi, so that at the end of the second one your sword will be in Guardia Alta.

4. Pass forward with your left foot and perform a *ritocco* of the buckler, getting into Guardia di Testa with your sword.

5. Pass forward with your right foot and perform a thrust-like montante[92] ending in Guardia Alta, then recover your right foot back near the left.

6. Perform this embellishment, rather than any of the ones described in the previous plays (it must be clear by now that every assalto has its own embellishment):

   a. Cut a fendente into the rim of your buckler while stepping back with your right foot.

   b. Let the sword go down, then up again into Guardia Alta, then perform another mulinetto behind the head like a turning circle (using your wrist).

   c. Pull your left foot near your right and give the buckler a good *ritocco*.

   d. Pass forward with your left foot, moving into Guardia di Testa.

   e. Pass forward with your right foot and deliver a thrust-like montante, ending in Guardia Alta, pulling your right foot near the left in the same tempo.

And as you come to blows with your opponent:

1. Pass forward with your right foot, delivering a mandritto that goes Sopra il Braccio and pull your right foot back near the left.

2. Immediately pass forward again with your right foot , delivering a half riverso into Guardia di Faccia, followed by two stramazzoni, the last of which ends in Porta di Ferro Stretta; let your head be well defended by the buckler.

---

92 This may be a strongly-ascending thrust.

3. Gather your right foot back near the left and deliver a montante into Guardia Alta.

4. Pass forward with your right foot, delivering a half mandritto that ends in Guardia di Faccia.

5. Strike two stramazzoni to his head, of which the last is a feint—that is, feint the stramazzone to hit him instead with a mandritto to the leg—with your sword ending in Porta di Ferro Larga.

6. Lift a falso that goes into Guardia Alta.

7. Pass back with your right foot and set yourself into Coda Lunga e Alta.

8. Gather back with your left foot, then pass forward (still with the left foot), pushing a thrust to his face.

9. Feint a stramazzone to his head, striking him instead with a riverso to the thigh followed by a thrust to the face and another stramazzone that ends in Porta di Ferro Stretta; ensure that your head is well defended by the buckler.

10. Gather your right foot forward near the left, and deliver a montante up to Guardia Alta.

Perform the embellishment as you have been taught.

11. Pass forward with your right foot, then with your left, pushing an ascending thrust to the opponent's face.

12. Pass forward with your right foot once again, delivering a riverso *ridoppio*[93] (that is, an ascending riverso) to his arms; then, deliver a fendente to his head that ends in Porta di Ferro Stretta.

13. Pass forward with your left foot and push a clever thrust to his face; as he lifts his sword to parry, strike his forward thigh with a riverso and go with your sword into Guardia di Testa.

14. Pass back with your left foot and strike a half mandritto into his sword-hand, ending in Porta di Ferro Larga.

15. Feint a falso to his sword; as he tries to void it, go under his blade with yours and push a thrust to his face. When he tries to parry your thrust, strike his right thigh with a riverso.

16. For your safety, strike his sword-hand with a falso, followed by a mandritto to the face ending in Porta di Ferro Larga.

17. Push a thrust to his sword-hand, letting your buckler cover your sword-hand.

18. Redouble two stramazzoni to his head.

19. Deliver a montante into Guardia Alta while gathering your right foot back near the left.

---

93 A ridoppio is a rising oblique cut delivered with the true edge.

Perform the embellishment as you have been taught.

20. Pass sideways with your left foot and deliver a mandritto that feints it is falling.[94]

21. Quickly pass forward with your right foot, and place your false edge under his blade.

22. Pass forward with your left foot, turn your hand and push a thrust to his face.

23. Pass forward with your right foot in a wide stance, redoubling two stramazzoni to his head, of which the last must end in Porta di Ferro Stretta; let your head be well defended by the buckler.

24. Gather your right foot back near your left and deliver a montante into Guardia Alta.

25. Pass forward with your right foot and deliver a mandritto to his leg that goes Sotto il Braccio.

26. Pass with your left foot towards his right side and deliver a riverso to his face. Let your right foot follow behind the left as you go into Coda Lunga.

27. Pass forward with your right foot, delivering an ascending falso into Guardia di Faccia.

28. Feint a riverso to his right temple, instead striking his forward leg with a mandritto that goes Sotto il Braccio; let your head be well-guarded by the buckler.

29. Pull your right foot back, then pass forward with your right foot delivering a riverso to the face going into Coda Lunga e Stretta.

30. Gather your right foot back near your left while lifting a montante into Guardia Alta.

Perform the embellishment as you have been taught.

31. Pass forward with your right foot, striking him with a mandritto that goes Sopra il Braccio, letting your right shoulder point towards the opponent's chest.

32. Deliver a fendente-like riverso[95] ending in Coda Lunga e Stretta and come back Sopra il Braccio with a falso to his hand that goes Sopra il Braccio; then, lift your hand into Guardia Alta.

33. Gather your right foot back near the left, and deliver a mandritto going Sotto il Braccio.

---

94   *Mandritto in sembiante di cadere*; this may be a mandritto that intentionally misses the target so that the action that follows may be executed, that is, placing the false edge under the opponent's sword, then performing a strong thrust with opposition.

95   Other Masters of the time would say a *riverso fendente*, that is, a descending true-edge cut going left to right (from the perspective of the swordsman delivering it).

34. Pass with your right foot towards his left side, and strike him with a falso that goes into Guardia di Faccia.

35. Pass forward with your left foot and feint a riverso to his right temple.

36. Quickly pass with your right foot towards his left side and deliver a fendente to his face going into Porta di Ferro Larga, letting your left foot follow behind the right;[96] ensure that your head is well defended by the buckler.

37. Gather your left foot back near your right, delivering a falso that ends in Guardia di Faccia.

38. Pass forward with your right foot, go with your sword into Guardia Alta and strike his head with a fendente, followed by two stramazzoni to the face, ensuring that your head is well defended by the buckler.

39. Pull your right foot back near the left and deliver a montante into Guardia Alta.

40. Pass forward with your right foot and deliver a fendente, ending in Guardia di Faccia.

41. Pass with your left foot towards his right side, delivering a stramazzone that ends in Cinghiara Porta di Ferro.

42. Pass forward with your right foot, feint a stramazzone to his head, while instead striking his leg with a mandritto that goes Sotto il Braccio.

43. Pull your right foot back and strike his sword-hand with a riverso, ensuring that your head be well defended by your buckler.

44. Pass forward with your right foot and deliver a falso ending in Guardia di Faccia.

45. Immediately pass forward with your left foot while feinting a mandritto, then strike him with a riverso.

46. Pass back with your left foot, and in the same tempo deliver a mandritto that ends in Guardia di Faccia.

47. Throw your right foot behind the left, turning your hand[97] to end in Coda Lunga e Alta.

48. Gather back with your left foot near your left,[98] then pass forward with your right foot while pushing a thrust to the opponent's face, followed by a fendente that does not go beyond the Guardia di Faccia.

---

[96] This (as well as the next step) may be a case where Manciolino mistakenly substitutes the right for the left foot. After a right-foot oblique pass ending in Porta di Ferro Larga, it should be the left foot following behind the right in a compass step; and subsequently, it should be the right foot that gathers back near the left (next step).

[97] Likely a mezza volta.

[98] Here is another example of mistaken substitution of the feet; this passage likely reads "Gather back with your left foot near your right..."

49. Pull your right foot back near the right and deliver a mandritto that goes Sotto il Braccio.

50. Pass with your left foot towards his right side and deliver an ascending falso that ends in Guardia di Faccia.

51. Pass forward with your right foot, going into Guardia Alta, then deliver a fendente to his head that finishes in Porta di Ferro Stretta. Ensure that your head is well protected by your buckler.

52. Pull your right foot back near the left, delivering a montante into Guardia Alta.

Perform the embellishment as you have been taught.

53. Pass forward with your right foot and deliver a less-than-finished mandritto[99] that goes Sopra il Braccio.

54. Pass with your left foot towards his right side, turning your buckler over your sword-hand and going with your sword into Cinghiara Porta di Ferro.

55. Pass forward immediately with your right foot and hit his blade with a falso, finishing in Guardia Alta; then quickly deliver a mandritto to his leg that ends in Sotto il Braccio. Ensure that your head is well defended by your buckler.

56. Pass back with your right foot and deliver a riverso to his sword-hand, ending with your sword in Coda Lunga e Larga.[100]

57. Pull your left foot back near the right, then pass forward with your right foot and push a thrust to his face.

58. Pass with your left foot towards his right side and feint a riverso.

59. Pass with your right foot towards his left side and deliver a fendente to his face, so that your sword ends in Porta di Ferro Larga; let your left foot follow behind the right.

60. Gather forward with your left foot while delivering a falso that ends in Guardia di Faccia, accompanying your sword-hand with your buckler.

61. Then immediately pass forward with your right foot and deliver a riverso to his face that ends in Coda Lunga e Stretta. Ensure that your head is well defended by the buckler.

62. Pass forward with your left foot and push a thrust to his face.

63. Pass forward with your right foot and redouble two stramazzoni to his head, ending the second one with your sword in Porta di Ferro Stretta.

---

[99] A different nomenclature for a *colpo imperfetto*.

[100] Here is another Bolognese guard that appears in passing in Manciolino, while not being included in the main ten guards.

64. Pull your right foot back near the left while delivering a montante into Guardia Alta.

Perform an embellishment as you have been taught.

65. Perform a *stretta* of the half sword by passing forward with your right foot without moving your sword or your buckler, then passing forward with your left foot in a wide stance, push a montante-like thrust that ends in Guardia di Faccia.

66. Pass forward with your right foot, feinting a mandritto to your head and striking his leg instead with a sideways cut.

67. Make yourself small under your sword, going to Guardia di Faccia, thus protecting yourself from the opponent's strike.

68. Pass with your left foot towards his right side, delivering a riverso to his right temple, letting your right foot follow behind the left and ensuring that your head is well defended by the buckler.

69. Push a thrust to his face and retreat with a backward-jump, keeping your sword in Coda Lunga e Alta.

70. Pass forward with your right foot and deliver a montante into Guardia Alta.

71. Recover your right foot back near the left and you will have finished the play.

As you wish to carry Victory back to the place where you started, start by going backward in this manner:

1. Pass back with your right foot, delivering a mandritto that goes Sotto il Braccio.

2. Pass back with your left foot, delivering a montante to your left side, ending in Guardia Alta.

3. Gather back with your right foot while delivering another montante, this one to your right side.

4. Pass back with your right foot and deliver a mandritto that goes Sotto il Braccio.

5. Pull your left foot back next to the right, withdraw your sword to your chest and place it Sopra il Braccio (over the buckler-arm).

6. Pass forward[101] with your left foot, performing a mulinetto to the outside of your arm, ending with your sword in Coda Lunga e Stretta.

7. Place your right foot so that your heel touches the tip of your left foot; lifting your sword in Guardia Alta in the same tempo, with your buckler well extended towards the opponent.

---

[101] Likely another clerical error, this should be a backward pass, also because it ends in Coda Lunga e Stretta (a right-foot-forward guard).

Book Three

Much more joyful than our martial plays are the assalti that rough-haired Satyrs conduct toward hunting Nymphs in the pages of poetry books. Those subjects are so fine that words compose themselves for the poet, in a sweet and ever-flowing style.[102]

When bards attempt to tell of goat-gods' wooly limbs, their horny brows, their gestures so licentious, words are not compos'd, but hues on canvas paint their rustic charge, while breathless Nymphs a-flee. One lifts her purple gown above her milky knee, as braids of golden hair cascade upon her chest, and quiet breezes blow and part her locks so fine. And others plunge in rivers sheer and fluid, where shelter lays (they hope) for their unsullied flow'r, Diana's ward. And others yet, now conquer'd by fatigue, in shrubs and bushes do their safety seek; their faces quite like blooms as Dawn begins to appear, the drops of pearly sweat they clear, with snow-white hands and fingers slight, regaining their lost wind.

You must forgive me, learned reader, for it is my lot in life to write about subjects not nearly as delightful as these. My subject does not carry anything but *mandritti, riversi, falsi*, thrusts and similar words which cannot be called by any other name if you want to make yourself understood in our art. Let us look, for instance, at the meaning of the word "to pass," which goes through my pen all the time as I write. While a fencer passes with his right or left foot, I can use the words *pass* as well as a great variety of synonyms.[103] Even as far as *right* goes, I can use the word *right, strong*, or *dominant*,[104] since men have more natural strength in their right side than in their left. Likely, the word *left* may be changed into *weak*[105] to avoid repetition, because there's nothing more detestable than the frequent occurrence of the same word in a sentence.

I concede that my choppy language will hardly please those whose chaste ears only hear the sweet and languid song of Philomena; but if these men are to behave like men, they must at least read this work with an eye to its rightful goal, and look elsewhere for more ornate writing.

Going back to our subject, I will devote this third book to the art of the half sword. As you fence against your opponent, you will often get to the narrow play or *strette* in such a way that it would be best for you to play at the half sword. But this requires a sharp mind and a great deal of art.

---

[102] This introduction makes an important point concerning language in early swordsmanship treatises. Some technical words may not be altered through synonyms, while others admit a few variations. In general, though, language in a book containing technical artistic instruction can never be as elevated as that in literary works, says Manciolino.

[103] Here, Manciolino lists a variety of synonyms and different spellings that have no real meaning other than "pass" in a fencing context. Rather than arbitrarily inventing words in English, I have opted to list them in the original in this footnote. The verbs are: *varcare, valicare, scorrere, scorgere, guidare, condurre il piede.*

[104] Manciolino uses the synonyms *dritto, forte* and *valido.*

[105] Manciolino uses two synonyms (the first of which means exactly "left"): *manco* and *debole.*

This type of play is first among all others.

He who does not understand it perfectly and does not have an excellent foundation in it will never be a good Master. No matter how good a fencer, how skilled in the defense and how quick with his hands, he will be unable to teach the true art to others, since the true art consists in being strongest and most resilient.[106] Rather than knowledgeable, these fencers should more aptly be considered to be lucky when they score a hit.

This third book is not divided into chapters, but rather in offenses and counters. Let it be also understood that I am speaking of fencing with sword and small buckler.

As you are at the *strette* of the half sword with your opponent, and you are to be the agent, you need to be very quick with your hands; if you are slow and lazy, you will always end up being the patient. You must also know that you can only find yourself at the half sword from two positions: that is, either true edge on true edge (meaning that your swords will be pointed at your[107] left shoulders) or false edge on false edge (meaning that your swords will be pointed at each-others' right shoulders).

There are therefore different attacks and defenses for each of these two situations. Let us start with what you can do from the position of false edge on false edge.

First Stretta, False Edge on False Edge

If you are in this situation, with the false edges touching each-other and you have the right foot forward, you can deliver a stramazzone-like sideways falso to his left temple. For your safety, you must then immediately pass back with your right foot (or dominant[108] foot, if you like!), delivering a riverso to his right temple.

Here is the counter to this action. As the opponent turns his stramazzone-like falso, immediately pass with your weak foot (or left foot, if you prefer!) towards his right side and deliver an ascending riverso to his right temple.

Second Stretta, False Edge on False Edge

If you are at the half sword and cannot strike him with the action described above, kick him in the stomach with your right foot and immediately pass back with the same foot, delivering a fendente to his head.

Here is the counter to this action. As the opponent kicks you, hit his shin with your buckler, which will effectively interrupt his design.

---

[106] Manciolino uses the word *fortissimo*, which is too vague in this context to translate with a single adjective. *Forte* can mean anything from strong, resilient, brawny, capable and even knowledgeable, all of which fit the context.

[107] Meaning each-other's.

[108] This is a clear (and humorous) allusion to the introduction to Book Three.

Third Stretta, False Edge on False Edge

If you are with the left foot forward, pass with your right foot towards his left side and feint a mandritto to his head; then drop your sword behind you, pass with your left foot towards his right side, thrust your head under his right arm, place your right hand between his thighs, lift him from the ground and let him fall backward behind your shoulders.

Here is the counter to this action. As the opponent feints the mandritto, do not respond in any way. But as he lets his sword fall to thrust his head under your arm, pass back with your right foot in a wide stance and deliver a riverso to his neck.

Fourth Stretta, False Edge on False Edge

If you have your right foot forward, feint a mandritto to his left temple, but let your sword instead turn mulinetto-like, immediately pass with your left foot towards his right side, and deliver a riverso to his right temple.

Here is the counter to this action. As he feints the mandritto, close your sword-hand and your buckler-hand together; as he passes with his left foot to deliver the riverso, pull your left foot behind the right and deliver a half mandritto to the left temple ending in a position not unlike Guardia Di Faccia; this will prevent him from hitting you with the riverso.

Fifth Stretta, False Edge on False Edge

If you have the right foot forward, place your sword-hand to the inside of his (going from below), and press down on his hand so much that you can wound him in the neck with your false edge.

Here is the counter to this action. As the opponent places his hand as described, use your hand to push his sword-arm towards his left, and this will prevent his action.

Sixth Stretta, False Edge on False Edge

If you have the right foot forward, pass with your left foot towards his right side, hit his sword-hand with your buckler-hand (to your outside), and finish with a riverso to his neck or head.

Here is the counter. As he passes forward with his left foot to strike you with his buckler-hand, hit him in the incoming arm with your buckler-rim.

Seventh Stretta, False Edge on False Edge

If you have your right foot forward, you can pass forth with your left foot in a wide stance and attack him with an ascending riverso; then immediately pass with your right foot to his left side and deliver a fendente-like mandritto,[109] letting your left foot follow behind the right.

---

[109] I.e., a *mandritto fendente*, a descending true-edge cut proceeding right to left (from the point of view of the person delivering it).

Here is the counter. As he passes forward with his left foot to strike you with the riverso, get into Guardia di Faccia with the buckler under your sword-hand, so that your buckler-hand touches your sword-hand and the latter is protected by the buckler. As he turns the fendente-like mandritto, pass back with your right foot and deliver a half mandritto to his sword-hand.

Eighth Stretta, False Edge on False Edge

If you have your left foot forward, pass with your right foot towards his left side, pull your sword back and under his and in the same tempo place your buckler under his sword-hand, striking him with a falso to the left side of his neck. Then, pass back with your left foot and place your sword in Guardia di Faccia, pass back with your right foot and deliver a pushed riverso to his right temple.

Here is the counter. As the opponent pulls his sword back and under yours, pull your right foot back and get into Guardia di Faccia.

Ninth Stretta, False Edge on False Edge

As you stand with your left foot forward, pass forward with your right foot, feinting a mandritto to his head. Then, perform the *Perugian Play*.[110] That is, throw away the sword and the buckler, grab the opponent firmly with both hands and let yourself fall on your hind end; then, shove your lifted feet side-by-side against his stomach, which will throw him behind your shoulders.

The counter is this. As he passes forward to feint the mandritto, pay attention and watch his hand for grips. As you see him letting go of his sword and buckler, pass back with your right foot and strike him in the head with a riverso.

Tenth Stretta, False Edge on False Edge

If you have the left foot forward, pass with your right foot towards his right,[111] hitting his blade with a strong mandritto; then, pass also to his right, but with your left foot, and deliver a riverso to his neck, letting your right foot follow behind the left.

Here is the counter to this action. As he passes forward to hit your blade with a mandritto, wait for it and hit his sword in turn, and when he passes to strike you with the riverso, turn a half mandritto to his face.

Eleventh Stretta, False Edge on False Edge

If you have the left foot forward, pass with your right foot towards his left side while feinting a mandritto, and instead strike his thigh with a nice riverso; leave your upper body open to invite an attack. As the attack comes, get your sword into Guardia di Testa and parry; then, use your buckler-hand to grab his sword from the inside of yours, while delivering a fendente to his head or a thrust to his face.

---

[110] Perugia is an Italian city in the region of Umbria.

[111] This is a cross-line pass.

Here is the counter. As the opponent passes to feint the mandritto, do not respond at all; but as he attacks your thigh with the riverso, turn your sword-point down and parry, delivering a fendente to the head as a riposte.

Twelfth Stretta, False Edge on False Edge

If you have your right foot forward, strike the opponent with a mandritto to the head. If he is a good fencer, he will hit into it, at which you will tilt your head[112] to make him think you are about to deliver a riverso, while instead striking him with the mandritto.

Here is the counter. As he feints a mandritto to your head, parry by delivering an ascending riverso going into Guardia di Testa; then, press down on his sword with your buckler-hand, while hitting his upper parts (wherever you see fit) with a riverso.

Thirteenth Stretta, False Edge on False Edge

If you have your right foot forward, feint a mandritto to his head, delivering instead a drilled-thrust-like riverso.

Here is the counter. As he performs the feint, do not move. As he delivers the riverso, pull your right foot back and go with your sword into Guardia di Faccia.

Fourteenth Stretta, False Edge on False Edge

If you have your right foot forward, pass forward with your left while executing a mezza volta with your sword-hand; while performing the mezza volta, push a thrust to his face.

Here is the counter. While the opponent passes forward with his left foot, quickly pass back with your left foot and get into Coda Lunga e Alta.

Fifteenth Stretta, False Edge on False Edge

If you have your right foot forward, feint a mandritto to the opponent's head; as the opponent attempts a parry, deliver a riverso to his thigh and set yourself into Guardia di Faccia.

Here is the counter. As the opponent performs the feint, do not move. Against the riverso to the thigh, step back with your right foot and strike a riverso into his sword-arm.

Sixteenth Stretta, False Edge on False Edge

If you have your right foot forward, feint a riverso to his head, giving him instead a mandritto to the flank[113] and setting yourself in Guardia di Faccia.

Here is the counter. As the opponent feints the riverso, step back with your right foot; as he attacks with the mandritto to your flank, mess up his sword-hand with a half mandritto, accompanying your cut with the buckler.

---

[112] This is a great insight into the style: since the whole body is often involved in the delivery of an attack, a feint can be executed with other than the sword—in this case, the head.

[113] This is a rare case in Italian swordsmanship of the period where a cut is directed at the body rather than the head, neck or limbs.

Seventeenth Stretta, False Edge on False Edge

If you have your right foot forward, place your buckler under the opponent's sword while passing with your left foot towards his right side and delivering a sideways mandritto to his right thigh. Then, let your right foot follow behind the left.

Here is the counter. As he tries to place his buckler under your sword, step back with your right foot and deliver a mandritto to his sword-hand, accompanied by your buckler.

Having described what you can do in the strette of the half sword when you are false edge on false edge, let us move on to the other way, that is, true edge on true edge. We will examine the respective offenses and the counters,[114] following the same order we used up to now. I would like to repeat that there is no other form of half-sword play than these two.[115]

First Stretta, True Edge on True Edge

If you have your swords true edge on true edge and you are to be the agent as you have your right foot forward, pass with your left foot towards the opponent's right side and deliver a pushed riverso to his right temple. Let your right foot follow behind the left.

Here is the counter. As he passes to strike the riverso, turn a half mandritto to his head, going up into Guardia di Faccia.

Second Stretta, True Edge on True Edge

If you have your right foot forward, pass with your left foot towards the opponent's right side, delivering an ascending riverso to his sword-arm; then, immediately step back with your left foot, delivering a mandritto to his face.

Here is the counter. As he passes to attack you with the riverso, place the buckler so as to defend from the attack from below; as he withdraws the left foot to deliver the mandritto, hit him in the right temple with a sideways riverso.

Third Stretta, True Edge on True Edge

If you have your right foot forward (which will be the starting point to all the attacks that follow, so that I can spare you some boredom by not repeating myself), turn a riverso to his right temple. If the opponent goes to parry, hit his sword with your hilt towards your outside, and deliver a fendente to his head.

Here is the counter. As he turns the riverso, parry it with the true edge; as he tries to hit your sword with his hilt, immediately lift your sword upwards thereby voiding his blow, and deliver a riverso to his head in the same tempo.

---

[114] Manciolino uses the terms *pro* and *contra* for "offenses" and "counters."

[115] Meaning true edge on true edge and false edge on false edge, as Manciolino stated at the opening of Book Three.

Fourth Stretta, True Edge on True Edge

Feint a riverso, then immediately pass with your left foot towards his right side and turn your pommel over his sword-hand (to your outside), press down on his hand so that you can strike his head with a riverso.

Here is the counter. As he feints the riverso, do not move. As he performs the turn of the pommel, quickly place your buckler under his sword and strike him in the thigh with a sideways riverso.

Fifth Stretta, True Edge on True Edge

Pass with your left foot towards his left side while feinting a riverso; then, pass back with your left foot and strike him with a fendente to the head.

Here is the counter. As he feints the riverso, do not move. As he turns the fendente to your head, deliver an ascending riverso that goes up into Guardia di Testa.

Sixth Stretta, True Edge on True Edge

Pass forward with your left foot towards his left side, into a wide stance, while cutting an ascending riverso to his sword-arm. Then, perform the following grapple. Feint a buckler-strike to his face; as he moves his head from fear, thrust your buckler-arm to the inside of his sword-arm and bind it, pulling it strongly and tightly to your left armpit. Then, pass back with your right foot, ensuring that he cannot strike you with his buckler.

Here is the counter. As he passes with the left foot as described to attack you with a riverso, extend your sword-hand forward (well covered by your buckler); as he feints the buckler-strike to your face, further extend your sword-hand (with your sword) forward to invite the bind; as he attempts to grab you, grasp his arm as it comes towards you, strongly pressing it downwards. The opponent will feel the pain from your clutching him and will let go of his buckler; at which point you can leisurely strike his face with a riverso.

Seventh Stretta, True Edge on True Edge

Feint a riverso, then immediately strike him with a mandritto to the leg and set yourself in Guardia di Faccia.

Here is the counter. As the opponent feints a riverso, do not move. As he attacks you with the mandritto, throw your right foot back and deliver a sideways mandritto to his sword-arm.

Eighth Stretta, True Edge on True Edge

Feint a riverso to the opponent's head, then pass with your left foot towards his right side while placing your buckler under his sword and delivering a mandritto to his leg. Let your right foot follow behind the left.

Here is the counter. As he feints the riverso, keep an eye to his hands, but do not move. As he passes with his left foot to attack you with a mandritto, step back with your right foot and deliver a half mandritto to his sword hand.

Ninth Stretta, True Edge on True Edge

Pass with your left foot towards his right side, hitting the opponent's right temple with a riverso; then immediately hit his face with the rim of your buckler.

Here is the counter. As he passes to strike you with a riverso, pull your right foot back and set yourself in Guardia di Faccia.

Tenth Stretta, True Edge on True Edge

Pass with your left foot towards the opponent's right side, delivering a riverso to his right temple. Then, somewhat withdrawing your left foot, feint a mandritto to his head, then step with your left foot towards his right side and strike his head with a riverso, letting your right foot follow behind the left.

Here is the counter. As the opponent passes to attack you with the riverso, parry with your true edge; as he feints the mandritto, place your sword into Guardia di Faccia; as he attacks you with the second riverso, throw your right foot towards his left side and strike his left temple with a half mandritto.

Eleventh Stretta, True Edge on True Edge

Deliver a riverso to his right temple and kick him in the stomach with your left foot. Then, recover your left foot back while giving him a mandritto to the head.

Here is the counter. As he delivers the riverso, parry with your true edge; as he delivers the kick, immediately strike his shin with the rim of your buckler, then defend against the mandritto by going into Guardia di Faccia.

Twelfth Stretta, True Edge on True Edge

Pass with your left foot towards the opponent's right side, into a wide stance, and feint a riverso; then withdraw your sword-hand, placing your buckler under his sword-hand and push a thrust to his face.

Here is the counter. As he feints the riverso, oppose it with your true edge. As he withdraws his sword to deliver the thrust, use the true edge again, to press the opponent's sword towards your left side, which will defend you from the thrust. Then, give him a falso to the face as soon as you can.

Thirteenth Stretta, True Edge on True Edge

Pass with your left foot towards the opponent's right side, delivering a sideways riverso to his right thigh and making yourself small into Guardia di Testa. Let your right foot follow behind the left.

Here is the counter. As he passes to deliver the riverso, step back with your right foot and deliver a riverso to his sword-arm.

Fourteenth Stretta, True Edge on True Edge

Pass with your left foot towards his right side, feinting a riverso to his head; then pass with your right foot towards his left side and strike his head with a mandritto. Let your right foot follow behind the left.[116]

Here is the counter. As he feints the riverso, close your sword together with your buckler; as he passes to give you the fendente, turn a riverso to his right temple.

Fifteenth Stretta, True Edge on True Edge

Pull your sword back and push a thrust to his right temple, accompanied by the buckler; let your right foot follow behind the left[117] to shield yourself against any dangerous blow.

Here is the counter. As he performs the thrust, hit it with your false edge, and strike him with a mandritto to the face.

Sixteenth Stretta, True Edge on True Edge

Pass with your left foot to the opponent's right side, into a wide stance, while grabbing his sword at mid-blade with your buckler-hand and striking his right temple with a riverso.

Here is the counter. As he passes to perform the grapple, strike his face with a half mandritto.

Seventeenth Stretta, True Edge on True Edge

Pass with your left foot towards his right side and turn a riverso to his right temple. Then, grab his sword at mid-blade with your buckler-hand, striking him in the face with your hand (from the inside), or giving him a good hair-pulling.

Here is the counter. As he comes forward to attack you with a riverso, parry by performing a mezza volta with your sword-hand; as he grasps your sword at mid-blade to strike your face with his hand, hit his incoming arm with the rim of your buckler, giving him also a mandritto to the face.

---

[116] Here is another possible mistake concerning the placement of the feet: after a right-foot oblique pass, it should be the left foot following behind the right with a compass step.

[117] This implies that the thrust may be accompanied by an oblique left-foot pass (i.e., a left-foot pass to the opponent's right side).

Book Four

Noble reader, I consider it necessary at this juncture to explain my earlier declaration that I would leave this work bare of any literary ornament. If you examine the matter closely, you can but admit that there are many things which we deem praiseworthy in one situation while considering them utterly unfit for another.

Indeed, who could fail to praise delicate manners, graceful deportment and the use of tasteful makeup in a beautiful woman? Yet, the same attributes observed in a young man would make us recoil. Or who could fail to express sweet approbation for a baby's first blabber? Yet, the same talk from an adult would cause us to laugh and doubt the person's sanity. Thus, we can say that something is laudable or despicable not in itself, but rather in relation to the person or thing of which it is an attribute.

Likewise, he who fails to praise the splendid colors of polished literature, the elegance of well-composed speech, and the harmony of poetry would be rightfully deemed insensible. Yet, it would be equally insensible to adopt the same form of speech in a topic for which it is unfit. Therefore, a wise writer always creates characters who speak and reply in a manner befitting their condition. It would not be proper for a mature person of years to either dress as an adolescent or flirt like one. Just as improper would be for a man of arms, rust-stained from the constant donning of armor, to utter debonair sounds with the same tongue that is so accustomed to debilitating thirst and hunger and to the dust that forever saturates the spacious martial field—unless that speech was the one delivered by the magnanimous Ajax against the sagacious Odysseus.[118]

That speech Ajax gave before all Grecian princes, in the occasion of a contest between the two heroes for the arms of great Achilles. Ajax displayed the disposition of a noble soldier, Odysseus that of a consummate orator. And even if Odysseus' speech had been despoiled of its persuasive tones, it would still have surpassed that of Ajax. Nay, it would have been like Diana stripped of her precious ornaments or like Venus standing next to Pales, the ever-nude and fair goddess of shepherds.[119]

With this, I wish to conclude that although I do not come before you as an orator, my speech will not be so rough as to be unworthy of comparison with that of other modern, more polished works—if not from its outside, at least underneath its surface.

Proceeding to my fourth labor, I will now write of the art of the *spada da filo* and *targa* or large buckler. The diligent understanding of this can also be applied to the *spada da gioco*. At the end of this fourth book, I will also include two more plays: that of two swords and that of single sword.

---

[118] Manciolino probably alludes to the speeches that Odysseus and Ajax delivered in Book IX of the *Iliad*, to persuade an irate Achilles to again take up arms on behalf of the Achaeans against Troy. Odysseus, known as a fine orator, delivered a long and ornate speech: "...and must we, Gods! Our heads inglorious lay/in Trojan dust, and this the fatal day?/Return, Achilles! Oh, return, though late/to save the Greeks and stop the curse of fate..." While Ajax, a man of arms, offers a much shorter and direct one: "...One woman slave was ravish'd from thy arms;/Lo, sev'n are offer'd, and of equal charms./Then hear, Achilles! Be of better mind;/Revere thy roof, and to thy guests be kind..." (Tr. Alexander Pope)

[119] The Goddesses mentioned are Diana (Gr. Artemis), goddess of hunting, Venus (Gr. Aphrodite), goddess of love and beauty, and Pales, a lesser deity guarding shepherds and livestock.

Chapter I

Get in a good guard with the sword and the large buckler, with your left foot forward, the buckler-arm well extended towards the opponent and your sword in Coda Lunga e Alta.

Gather your right foot forward near the left, then step forward with your left foot, without delivering any attacks. As you press[120] the opponent in this fashion, he will be forced to do one of two things: either attack you or retreat. Let us assume that he attacks you with a thrust; at this, you can do many counters:

1. Pass with your right foot towards his left side, delivering a riverso to the sword-arm in that tempo and letting your left foot follow behind the right; then, keep yourself safe by passing back with your right foot and setting yourself in Coda Lunga e Alta as above.

2. Or, you can throw your left foot towards his left, while jamming your false edge under his incoming attack; pass with your right foot towards his left side and deliver a mandritto to his left leg, letting your left foot follow behind the right. Then, throw your right foot back and perform a mezza volta with your sword-hand, which will get you into the initial guard.

3. You could also pass with your right foot towards his left side, pushing a thrust to his flank and letting your left foot follow behind the right; then, pass back with your right foot and comfortably recover in the initial guard.

4. You could also pass with your right foot forward and somewhat to the opponent's left, jamming your false edge (accompanied by your buckler) under his incoming thrust; then, immediately strike his left leg with a riverso. Recover by passing back with your right foot and placing your sword in Guardia di Faccia, and finish by setting yourself in the initial guard.

5. Or, you could pass with your right foot forward and somewhat towards the opponent's left side, opposing his thrust with your true edge; then, turn a riverso to his face while passing back with your right foot. For your defense, end by pushing a thrust in Guardia di Faccia and recovering in Coda Lunga e Alta.

This finishes the counters you can perform to the opponent's thrust.

Following are the possible counters to an action in which the opponent delivers a thrust to strike you with a mandritto.[121] Let us assume that both fencers start in Coda Lunga e Alta with their left foot forward.

1. Against the thrust, you can deliver a half mandritto to his sword-hand, ensuring that your head is well defended by your buckler and finishing with your sword in Cinghiara Porta di Ferro. As he delivers the mandritto to your head, immediately pass forward with your right foot and parry by getting into

---

[120] *Stringere il nimico*; this means advancing against him in such a way as to force retreat or a response. *Pressing* is an adequate rendition of the meaning of this word in our context.

[121] To the head or to the leg, as Manciolino specifies in the counters.

Guardia di Testa; riposte with a sideways mandritto to his legs. Then, pass back with your right foot and turn your sword-hand, ending in Coda Lunga e Alta with your left foot forward.

2. You could also gather back with your left foot, then step forward with your right foot, jamming your true edge against his incoming thrust; when he turns the mandritto to your leg, place your sword under your buckler on the opponent's right side, thus parrying his attack. Afterwards, strike a sideways riverso to his right leg, then pass back with your right foot while pushing a thrust in Guardia di Faccia for your defense; end in Coda Lunga e Alta.

3. Or, you can pass back with your left foot while delivering a mandritto to his sword-hand ending in Porta di Ferro Larga; as he delivers the mandritto (to your head), parry with a falso while passing somewhat forward with your right foot, and deliver a riverso to his leg. Then, pass back with your right foot while pushing a thrust under your buckler into Guardia Di Faccia for your defense, and end in Coda Lunga e Alta.

4. You could also pass with your right foot towards his left side, parry his thrust with your buckler and deliver a mandritto to his leg, letting your left foot follow behind the right. Then, pass back with your right foot, turning your hand and setting yourself in your initial guard.

5. You could also pass with your right foot towards his right side, jamming your true edge into the incoming thrust and immediately turning a riverso to his head, which will prevent him from delivering his mandritto. Then, pass back with your right foot and push a thrust to his face, pulling your body back with agility, and recovering into Coda Lunga e Alta.

6. Or, you could strike his hand with an ascending falso while he delivers the thrust, ending in Guardia di Faccia; as he attacks with the mandritto, pass with your right foot towards his left side while hitting his sword-arm with a mandritto, letting your left foot follow behind the right;[122] then, turn your sword hand and you will be in the initial guard.

Chapter II

If the opponent delivers a thrust, gathers back with his left foot and passes forward with his right foot to attack you with a mandritto or a fendente, you can perform the following counter.

Do not move when he delivers the thrust; as he attacks with the mandritto, hit into it while going into Guardia di Testa with your right foot forward, and strike his leg with a mandritto. Then, pass back with your right foot and turn your hand as you know, recovering in the guard we have so often named.

---

[122] At this point, there may be an additional backward pass not mentioned by Manciolino, which would place you again with the left foot forward.

Chapter III

If the opponent delivers a thrust to attack you with a riverso to your face or leg, keep your eyes to his sword-hand.

As he delivers the thrust, pass forward with your right foot and parry with your false edge.

If he delivers the riverso to your head, pass forward with your left foot and parry with your true edge, ensuring that your head is well-defended by your buckler. Then, withdraw your sword-hand, push a thrust to his face, retreat with a backward jump and recover in Coda Lunga e Alta.

If he instead delivers the riverso to your leg, pass forward with your left foot, turning your true edge against the riverso (with your point down), push a thrust to his face, jump back and recover in Coda Lunga e Alta.

Chapter IV

Now that I have listed what you can do from Coda Lunga e Alta, I want to continue by talking about the attacks and counters from Coda Lunga e Stretta (right foot forward). Let me declare that there is no guard that is safer for the defense and more apt for the offense than this one.

If you want to press your adversary in this guard, gather forward with your left foot and pass forward with your right foot. As you press him this way, he will be forced to do one of two things: either attack you or retreat—and if he gives ground, he does so with shame.

Let us say he passes forward with his left foot and thrusts with the goal of disrupting you, then attacks you with a mandritto or any other blow he chooses.

Against the thrust, pass back with your right foot and set your sword in Cinghiara Porta di Ferro. As he attacks you with a mandritto (or another blow), immediately pass forward with your right foot and parry with a falso; riposte with a riverso to the right leg. Protect yourself by pushing a thrust to his face from under your buckler.

From there, pass back with your right foot in a wide stance, turning your sword so that the point is aimed at the opponent's face; push another thrust while retreating with a sprightly jump. Finish by recovering into Coda Lunga e Stretta with your right foot forward.

Chapter V

As you and your opponent stand in Coda Lunga e Stretta with your right foot forward and the opponent passes with his left foot and pushes a thrust to then attack you with a mandritto, parry the thrust with the true edge. Against the mandritto, push a thrust in Guardia di Faccia, thus defending against his blow. Then, pass with your left foot towards his right side, while delivering a riverso to his right thigh. From there, push a thrust to his face while retreating with a jump, and recover in Coda Lunga e Stretta with your right foot forward.

But let us stipulate that after the thrust, the opponent does not attack with a mandritto, but rather with a riverso to your head.

Pass forward with your right foot[123] and parry his attack with your true edge, ensuring that your head is well defended by your buckler. Then, pass with your right foot towards his left side while striking his left thigh with a mandritto, letting your left foot follow behind the right. For your safety, pass back with your right foot, turning your hand so that you are in Coda Lunga e Stretta[124] with your left foot forward. Pass back two or three times, then pass forward with your right foot and set yourself in Coda Lunga e Stretta.

If the opponent's riverso is not to your head but rather to your leg, pass forward with your left foot and parry with the true edge with your point down. After that, deliver a thrust to his flank and retreat with a backward jump. If you do not want to jump, it is enough to pass backward three or four times and recover into Coda Lunga e Stretta.

Chapter VI

If the opponent delivers a mandritto to your head, pass back with your right foot and hit his arm with a mandritto, ending in Cinghiara Porta di Ferro, ensuring that your buckler effectively guards your head.

Then, pass back with your left foot and turn your sword-hand, thus ending as usual in Coda Lunga e Stretta with your right foot forward.

Chapter VII

If the opponent delivers a thrust, a mandritto or a riverso, defend against any of these blows with a sideways falso to his sword-arm. Do not go beyond Guardia di Faccia, and ensure that your head is well-defended by your buckler. Then, recover in the initial guard.

If he attacks your right leg with a mandritto, immediately pass with your left foot towards his right side, jamming your false edge under your buckler and parrying his attack. Then, quickly deliver a riverso to his right leg, followed by a good thrust to the face. As soon as you finish the thrust, retreat with a nice jump, then pass forward with your right foot recovering in Coda Lunga e Stretta.

Chapter VIII

Now that I have exhausted the fine and masterful actions that can be done from Coda Lunga e Alta and from Coda Lunga e Stretta with the right foot forward, I still need to talk about two other guards for this mode of combat. I must explain this to the reader, because there are many ways to attack and defend from these two guards, which are the Cinghiara Porta di Ferro and the Porta di Ferro Stretta.

---

[123] A likely mistake; at this point in the action (and before another right-foot pass in the next sentence), it should be the left foot that passes forward. This is also confirmed in the next paragraph.

[124] Perhaps Manciolino means Coda Lunga e Alta, although this is practically identical to a Coda Lunga e Stretta with the left foot forward.

Let us begin with the first of these two guards. If you are both armed with the *spada da filo* and the large buckler or targa and are in Cinghiara Porta di Ferro, each of you can start the action. But if you are looking for victory, you must by no means be the one who starts the action, but rather stand in guard with subtle vigilance.

If the opponent passes forward with his right foot and pushes a thrust to attack your head with a mandritto, parry the thrust with your false edge without moving your feet. As he delivers the mandritto to your head, quickly pass forward with your sword in Guardia di Testa and parry. Then, riposte to his leg with a mandritto while keeping your head well-defended by your buckler. Pass back with your right foot while pushing a thrust into Guardia di Faccia, then recover in Cinghiara Porta di Ferro.

But if the opponent pushes a thrust to attack you with a mandritto to your leg, parry the thrust with your false edge. Against his attack to your leg, pass back with your left foot while striking his sword-arm with a mandritto of your own; then, retreat to safety by passing back two or three times and recovering in the aforementioned guard.

If instead he passes forward with his right foot and pushes a thrust to attack your head with a mandritto or fendente, parry the thrust with your false edge. Against his next blow, pass back with your left foot and strike his arm with a half mandritto; then, similarly passing back with your left foot,[125] you will recover in Cinghiara Porta di Ferro.

If he passes forward with his right foot and delivers the thrust to strike your leg with a mandritto, parry the thrust with your false edge. As he turns the mandritto, immediately pass with your right foot towards his right side placing your false edge under the mandritto in such a way that it is right under your buckler, and give him a riverso to the thigh. For your safety, pass back with your right foot while pushing a thrust to his face, and retreat with a backward jump. Then, recover into Cinghiara Porta di Ferro.

If, instead, he were to pass with his right foot and thrust, then attack you with a riverso to the face, parry the thrust with a falso, making sure it does not go beyond Guardia di Faccia. As he turns the riverso to your head, pass back with your left foot in a wide stance, and ensure that your head is well-defended by your buckler. Then, deliver a sideways mandritto to his sword-hand, pass back with your right foot and recover into Cinghiara Porta di Ferro.

If, under another scenario, he were to pass with the right foot and thrust, then attack you with a riverso to the leg, parry the thrust with the falso, as you did before; pass back with your left foot and hit his sword-arm with a half riverso. Then, pass back with your right foot and recover into Cinghiara Porta di Ferro.

---

[125] It should be "right foot."

Chapter IX

In this chapter, I will speak of the attacks that can be done if you and the opponent stand in Porta di Ferro Stretta, armed as I have specified above.[126]

If you want to press your opponent as you stand with your right foot forward, gather forward with your left foot, then step forward with your right.

If the opponent pushes a thrust[127] to then attack you with a mandritto, riverso or fendente to the head, parry the thrust with the usual falso; as he passes forward with his right foot to attack you with one of the blows I have listed, pass back with your right foot and deliver a sideways half mandritto to his sword-arm.[128] Then, pass back with your left foot and recover in Coda Lunga e Stretta.

If he instead pushes a thrust with a left-foot pass to attack your forward leg with a mandritto, parry the thrust with a falso, as I have said before. And while he passes with his right foot to deliver the mandritto, pass back with your right foot and also deliver a mandritto, to the inside of his sword-arm. For your safety, pass back with your left foot and recover in Porta di Ferro Stretta.

But if he pushes the thrust with a left-foot pass, passes with his right foot and attacks you with a mandritto or fendente to the head, parry the thrust by passing back with your right foot and going into Cinghiara Porta di Ferro. As he passes again to deliver the mandritto or fendente, pass forward with your right foot and deliver a sideways ascending falso to his sword, followed by a riverso to the leg. Then, for your safety, pass back with your right foot while pushing a thrust to his face under your buckler. Lastly, pass back with your left foot and recover in Porta di Ferro Stretta.

If he instead pushes the thrust with a left-foot pass, then passes again with the right foot to attack you with a mandritto to the leg, parry the thrust with a falso, as usual. As he passes to deliver the mandritto, pass with your left foot to his right side and jam your false edge under your buckler, thus parrying the incoming blow. Then, riposte with a riverso to the leg, followed by a thrust to the face as you jump backward. Recover in Porta di Ferro Stretta.

But if he attacks you with a riverso to the head after pushing the thrust with a left-foot pass, then parry the thrust with a falso, and without any footwork. And while he passes to deliver the riverso, pass forward with your left foot and defend by performing a mezza volta with your sword-hand; ensure that your head is well-defended by your buckler. Then, push your buckler against the opponent's sword while delivering a thrust to his face or chest (as you prefer). Lastly, retreat with a backward jump and recover in Porta di Ferro Stretta.

---

[126] That is, with the *spada da filo* and the large buckler or targa.

[127] The right-foot pass Manciolino describes after this implies that the thrust is accompanied by a left-foot pass. This is confirmed in the next paragraph.

[128] The text mistakenly reads "a sideways half mandritto to his sword-buckler." *Braccio* (arm) and *brocchiero* (buckler) are sufficiently similar words for the mistake to have gone unnoticed.

If his thrust with a left-foot pass was instead the prelude to a riverso to your leg, parry the thrust by passing with your left foot towards his right side and delivering a falso that does not go beyond Guardia di Faccia. As he attacks you with the riverso to the leg, pass forward with your right foot and turn an ascending half riverso with your point down (thereby parrying), then hit his sword-arm with a sideways mandritto while your head is guarded by the buckler. Lastly, pass back with your right foot and go with your sword into Guardia di Faccia, then pass back with your left and recover in Porta di Ferro Stretta.

Chapter X

I have now given you all that you can do (strictly in the art) from the aforementioned four guards while armed with the sword and large buckler or targa. For brevity's sake, I have not mentioned some of the actions that, although possible, are not quite as artistic. Now, however, I will include them in this separate chapter, starting with the Coda Lunga e Alta (which is the first guard we examined in this weapon-combination), and finishing in Porta di Ferro (which is the fourth and last).

From the Coda Lunga e Alta (left foot forward), you can push a thrust, feint a riverso to the head and strike him in the leg with a mandritto.

You can also push a thrust with a right-foot pass, feint a mandritto to his head but strike him with a riverso to the leg.

You can also push a thrust (also with a right-foot pass), and passing with your left foot to his right side, strike a mandritto to his leg; let your head be well-defended by your buckler, and let your right foot follow behind the left.

You can also push a thrust without any footwork, then gather back with your left foot, pass forward with your right and deliver a mandritto, a fendente or a riverso (as you prefer).

You can also deliver a half mandritto to his sword-hand, and get back with a riverso to the leg—without any footwork.

Or, you can deliver an ascending falso to his sword-hand, without any footwork.

Or, you may push an overhand thrust accompanied by a right-foot pass, ending in Porta di Ferro Larga; then perform a falso and mandritto, followed by falso and riverso. You could also deliver a falso that goes into Guardia di Faccia, pass forward with your left foot,[129] perform a mezza volta with your sword-hand and push a thrust to his face or chest. Actually, this is a very good attack against a left-handed fencer; you would be well defended against any of his attacks.

If a left-handed fencer attacks your leg, you should do the following. Pass forward with your left foot,[130] turn your point down (thereby parrying), and push a thrust to his face.

---

[129] It is unclear whether this is a continuation of the previous action, or another along the list of alternative attacks you may perform from Coda Lunga e Alta. In the second case, the left-foot pass is either an editorial error or must be preceded by an implied right-foot pass.

[130] This is another case of a possible mistake (where the passing foot may be the right) since it is implied that the initial guard is the Coda Lunga e Alta, i.e., with the left foot forward.

If the left-handed fencer attacks you with a mandritto, hit his incoming hand with a riverso. And if he attacks you with a riverso, hit his hand with a mandritto.

These are the rules to use against a left-hander, making sure that you always step against his sword.

Coming back to right-handed fencers, if the opponent attacks you with a mandritto to the head, pass back with your left foot and deliver a mandritto to his sword-hand.

If he delivers a mandritto to your leg, pass back with your left foot and hit his sword-hand with a half mandritto.

Always from Coda Lunga e Alta (left foot forward), you can push a thrust without footwork, gather back with your left foot while extending your sword backward, pass forward with the right and attack with an overhand thrust. Then, gather back with your right foot, your sword Sotto il Braccio, then pass forward with your left foot and push a punta riversa to his face; pass with your right foot to his left side and attack his head or his forward leg with a mandritto, or with a riverso, if it serves you better.

Chapter XI: The Play of Two Swords

Since the play of two swords, one in each hand, is quite advantageous and striking, this chapter will deal with the actions that the art calls for in this weapon combination.

Begin the play by standing on one side of the salle, facing your opponent (with whom you will fight). Put your right foot somewhat ahead of the left, the right sword in Porta di Ferro Stretta and the left in Guardia di Testa.

1. Pass with your right foot somewhat obliquely to your left, then pass similarly with your left foot, performing falso and riverso with your right sword (ending in Guardia di Testa) and falso and mandritto with your left sword (ending in Porta di Ferro Stretta); let your right foot follow behind the left.

2. Pass forward with your right foot while doing falso and riverso with your left sword (ending in Guardia di Testa) and falso and mandritto with your right (ending in Porta di Ferro).

3. Pass with your right foot towards the opponent's left side,[131] then forward with your left foot, doing falso and riverso with your right sword (ending in Guardia di Testa) and falso and mandritto with your left (ending in Porta di Ferro Stretta); let your right foot follow behind the left.

This ends the entry into play; following are the actions against the opponent and the return from play that places you where you started. This follows a similar order as the sword-and-buckler assalti I included in Book Two.

---

[131] Since this pass follows a right-foot pass, Manciolino may be meaning an oblique step (accrescimento) of the forward foot.

Having arrived near the opponent, you will attack him by doing the following:

1. Pass forward with your right foot delivering a thrust to the face followed by a riverso to the leg, ending with your right sword in Coda Lunga e Stretta and your left in Guardia di Testa.

2. Pass with your left foot towards his right side, delivering a fendente to the head with your left sword, ending in Porta di Ferro Stretta; let your right foot follow behind the left.

3. From there, push a thrust with both swords, crossed (for your safety) with your right sword above your left sword.

4. Pass with your right foot to his left side, delivering a mandritto to his head with your right sword (ending in Porta di Ferro Stretta), while your left sword gets into Guardia di Testa; let your left foot follow behind the right.

5. Pass with your right foot towards his right side, then with your left; meanwhile, do falso and riverso with your right sword (ending in Guardia di Testa) and falso and mandritto with your left (ending in Porta di Ferro Stretta); let your right foot follow behind the left.

6. Pass forward with your right foot, delivering a thrust with your right sword.

7. Pass with your left foot towards his right side, delivering a sideways mandritto to his right temple with your left sword, ending in Porta di Ferro Stretta, while your right sword ends in Guardia di Faccia; let your right foot follow behind the left.

8. Pass forward with your right foot and push a thrust to the opponent's face accompanied by a mandritto ending in Porta di Ferro Stretta, while your left sword gets into Guardia di Testa.

9. Immediately pass forward with your left foot and deliver a thrust to the opponent's face with your left sword.

10. Pass with your right foot towards the opponent's left side, delivering a mandritto to the opponent's left temple with your right sword (ending in Porta di Ferro); let your left foot follow behind the right and place your left sword in Guardia di Testa.

11. If the opponent ripostes with:

    a. A mandritto to your head delivered with his right sword, hit into his attack with your left sword, and deliver a thrust to his chest with your right sword.

    b. A riverso,[132] parry it with your right sword, while striking his head with a mandritto to the face delivered with your left sword.

---

[132] Presumably also with his right sword, given the order of the actions.

     c. A mandritto with his left sword, parry it with the true edge of your right sword, delivering a fendente to the face with your other sword.

     d. A riverso with his left sword, parry it with the true edge of your left sword, pushing a thrust to the face with your other weapon.

12. Gather back with your left foot, pass forward with your right while doing falso and riverso with your right sword and delivering a half mandritto with your left sword, ending in Guardia di Faccia.

13. Gather back with your right foot, and pass forward with your left, while pushing a thrust to his face with your left sword.

14. Pass with your right foot to the opponent's left, while delivering a mandritto that ends in Porta di Ferro Stretta, and let the left foot follow behind the right while your left sword gets into Guardia di Testa.

Once you finish the play, do the following to elegantly return to the corner of the salle where you started:

1. Pass back with your right foot and do falso and riverso with your right sword, ending in Guardia di Testa, while your left sword does falso and mandritto ending in Porta di Ferro Stretta.

2. Pass back with your left foot and do falso and mandritto with your left sword, lifting it into Guardia di Testa, while your right sword also does falso and mandritto but ends in Porta di Ferro.

3. Pass back with your right foot and do falso and riverso with your right sword, ending in Guardia di Testa, while your left sword does falso and mandritto, ending in Porta di Ferro Stretta. Thus you will end this beautiful retreat from play.

Chapter XII: The Play of Single Sword

When you are about to fence your opponent with the *spada da filo*, set yourself with the right foot forward and the sword in Porta di Ferro Stretta. Then, without delivering any sort of attack, press your opponent in this manner: gather forward with your left foot, and then step forward with your right. Thus provoked, the opponent will see himself compelled to either deliver an attack or retreat.

If he attacks you with a thrust, hit into it with your false edge and turn a half riverso to his thigh. Then, defend yourself by delivering an ascending falso to his sword-hand (making sure that you do not pass the Guardia di Faccia) and deliver another cut ending in Porta di Ferro Stretta.

But if he attacks with a thrust to your face in order to then strike you with a mandritto or riverso, parry his thrust with a falso; then, if his mandritto comes to your head, parry it by going into Guardia di Testa and respond with a similar blow to his head or leg—as you wish.

Your opponent could also attack you with a riverso or a mandritto to the leg. If it is with a mandritto, pull your right foot back and cut into his sword-hand with a half mandritto. Instead, if he attacks you with the riverso, pull your right foot back while delivering a half riverso to his sword-arm; then, recover in Porta di Ferro Stretta.

He could also push a thrust to strike your head or leg with a riverso. First, let us suppose that the riverso is to the head. Parry the thrust with the false edge without moving your feet. When he delivers the riverso, pass forward with your left foot and parry by performing a mezza volta with your hand; then, pass with your right foot toward his left side and deliver a mandritto to his head or leg (as you wish). Finish by letting your left leg follow behind the right. Let us now suppose that his riverso is to your leg. Defend by passing forward with the left foot and turning your point down; then, push a thrust of your own to his flank and immediately retreat by jumping backwards and recovering in Porta di Ferro Stretta.

If he attacks your upper parts with a mandritto or riverso fendente, or with a thrust, you can parry any of these blows with a falso, provided that you do not pass the Guardia di Faccia. Then, immediately pass forward while turning your hand, and push a thrust to your opponent's face or chest—as you prefer. Alternatively, after parrying with the falso, you can let loose a mandritto to his face and let it descend so that it hits his arms and chest: if you choose to deliver this stroke, accompany it with an accrescimento of your right foot. This is among the unique defenses that can be effected in this type of play.

Book Five

It often happens in lavish but unorganized banquets that all dishes are presented in their copious bounty at the same time, causing the diners to declare themselves full without touching any other fare; and causing the same to silently blame the servers who, either wanting to spare themselves the toil of carrying full plates too many times, or wanting to eat at the same time as the invitees, do so much injury to their guests.

Not wanting to make the same mistake, dear reader, I have abstained from offering you every subject right at the beginning; rather, I have served to you individual books (not unlike different courses), each with a prologue through which I can pique your taste for the subject to come, as well as defend myself against accusations as I am about to do.

You see, there are many who ignorantly state that my work is imperfect, since it fails to include instruction on how to challenge your opponent to fight those just duels that may cause warriors to enter mortal combat.[133] This subject deals with the choice of a place, the election of weapons, and similar absurdities. I say absurdities because it is absurd that anyone should consider them to be within the strict field of the swordsman, for whom this subject is as foreign as the orbit of the sun and the moon.[134]

So, I respond to these accusations by saying that, as each of the five senses has a single object, so is it impossible to have more than one subject in one art. For instance, the faculty of sight can only have color as an object; hearing can only have sound; taste can only have flavor, and so on. It would be silly to say that the function of the ears is not only to hear but also to see and to taste; similarly, it would be silly to suggest that the art of fencing consists not only in the virtue of blows, but also in the reasons that may move us to combat.

Who would be so blind not to see that "fencing" comes from "fence," that is to say, "defense,"[135] thus immediately understanding what the subject should be: the knowledge of attacks and defenses? If our art were also to comprise the reasons that move the different parties in a duel, the election of weapons and of the mode of combat, it would need another name than "fencing." It would be better named "fencing law" or "jurisprudence," or better yet "Imperial law."

You ignorant, blunt-witted minds, do you not see the error in which you fall? To hell with your laws; leave those to lawyers! If you know what fencing is, speak only of what pertains to our art—that is, of the great judgment one must possess as he defends against the opponent while offending him. Then, if you want to learn about the law and talk about it, be my guest, but do so as experts in the law, not as experts in fencing.

---

[133] Ironically, 19th-century British fencing historian Egerton Castle wrote in his 1885 *Schools and Masters of Fence* that "Manciolino's text is so much filled up by wise dissertations on the rules of honour and way of picking and deciding quarrels in a gentlemanly manner, that very little actual 'fencing' has found its way into his little work." This justly prompted ridicule from contemporary Italian fencing historians, who accused Castle of not having even read Manciolino's work.

[134] In 16th-century Italy, there was a strict distinction made between the *duellatore* (he who fights the duel) and the *duellista* (he who studies dueling rules and jurisprudence). Manciolino is saying that inserting a section that would be of interest to the latter is out of the scope of a swordsmanship book.

[135] In the original, these three terms are *arte schermitoria, schermire* and *difendere*.

It is possible to look at the same object from different perspectives—as for instance a philosopher, a doctor and an astrologer can look at the human body. The philosopher will see the body as a meeting of matter and soul. The doctor will recognize the four elements in it, and see which trumps the others when illnesses happen. Also, the doctor will consider the individual body, while the philosopher will examine the body as a universal concept. The astrologer, too, will look at the individual body, but will investigate under which celestial influence it was born. It would therefore not be appropriate for a doctor to look at illnesses and elements while adding considerations about celestial influences; if he were to do so, he would no longer speak as a doctor, but as an astrologer.

In the same manner, a lawyer and a fencer will look at combat from different points of view. The former will examine whether a cause is just and who gets the election of arms. The latter will see in which guard one is safest and with which blow he can best attack. It is actually more appropriate for a doctor to speak of astrology (since the two sciences have some relation) than for a fencer to do so about civic jurisprudence or Imperial law.

There is one regard in which fencing is similar to medicine: medicine starts where philosophy ends, just as fencing begins where jurisprudence ends. The lawyer's role stops at the reasons behind a duel and the justice of its taking place; that of the fencer starts when he takes the stipulated weapon in his hand. This is similar to the role of a writer, who uses the paper only after the paper-maker manufactures it. When he has a pen in his hand, the writer does not concern himself with the type of pulp used for the sheet on his desk. And as it can often happen that a writer uses paper of poor quality (for lack of a better product), so can a fencer move his weapon without much good judgment. It is therefore not jurisprudence that makes fencing good, but rather the knowledge of defenses and offenses. It is clear that the subject of our art is nothing more than the knowledge of fencing actions.

So, if I write a book on fencing in which I explain actions to the satisfaction of the art, what exactly is it that am I leaving out? Where exactly is it that I am going wrong? What exactly am I failing to disclose that pertains to our art? No, it is those who are so presumptuous as to include such blabber in a fencing work who are going wrong. And "blabber" is the only word we can use to describe what they write, since they are clearly oblivious of the rule that Aristotle gives in the first book of his *Posterior Analytics*,[136] where he states that it is wrong to go from genus to genus—that is, from one subject to another.

Going back to our purpose, this fifth book is divided into four plays. The first and second are for *spada da filo* and cape, with the first half dedicated to one-on-one combat, the rest to two-on-two. The next play is for the *spada da filo* in the right hand and the dagger in the left. The fourth is for the *spada* and *rotella*. Let us therefore start with the fist chapter, in which I will explain what follows.

---

[136] Aristotle, *Posterior Analytics*, Book I, 7: "It follows that we cannot in demonstrating pass from one genus to another. We cannot, for instance, prove geometrical truths by arithmetic." (Tr. G. R. C. Mure)

Chapter I: The Play of Sword and Cape

If you happen to be wearing a cape, let it fall off your upper right arm all the way down to the middle of your left arm. Then, turn your left hand to its outside,[137] gathering your fallen cape over your left arm, while unsheathing the sword with your other hand and setting yourself in Coda Lunga e Alta, your left foot elegantly forward.

If your opponent happens to be in the same guard:

1. Press him smartly by advancing, and he will have to either attack you or retreat.

2. If he attacks you with a thrust pushed with his left foot forward, pass with your right foot towards his left side, answering with a fendente-like riverso to his sword-arm, and letting your left foot follow behind the right; then, pass back and recover into Coda Lunga e Alta with your left foot forward.

3. Pass forward with your right foot and push a half thrust. Then, deliver a half riverso to the opponent's cape-hand, without moving your sword from there. This is because after you deliver this blow, the opponent will certainly deliver a thrust, a mandritto, or a fendente:

   a. If he attacks with a thrust, parry it downwards with your true edge and deliver a *punta riversa* to his chest or a riverso to his face.

   b. If he attacks with a mandritto or a fendente, pass forward with your left foot, parry with your cape and deliver a thrust to the opponent's flank.

   c. Then, retreat with a backward jump and recover in Coda Lunga e Alta.[138]

4. If the opponent (in the same guard) pushes a thrust with his left foot forward, gathers back with the left and passes forward with the right while attacking you with a mandritto to the head, do not move when he delivers the thrust. As he attacks with the mandritto, pass back with your left foot while hitting his sword-hand with a mandritto. Then, pass back with your right foot and perform a mezza volta with your hand, recovering into Coda Lunga e Alta.

5. If he is in the same guard and attacks you with a thrust, a mandritto or a fendente, defend against any of these by stepping with your left foot to his left side, lowering your point, then lifting it again in a wheel-like motion, thereby "picking up" any of these attacks.[139] Then, pass with your right foot towards the opponent's left side and deliver a mandritto to his head or leg, letting your left foot follow behind the right. Lastly, pass back with your right foot, turn your hand, and you will again be in Coda Lunga e Alta.

---

[137] Meaning counterclockwise, so that the excess fabric of the cape falls to the outside (i.e., the left) of your arm.

[138] It is unclear whether this retreat and recovery pertains only to point (b) or to both points (a) and (b).

[139] This action is similar to a circular parry.

6. As a probing action,[140] if the opponent is reluctant to leave his guard, you can push a half-thrust with a right-foot pass, followed by a half riverso to the thigh; then, wait for his riposte.

    a. If he ripostes with a thrust, parry it downwards with your true edge, then immediately deliver a *punta riversa* to his chest or a riverso to the face.

    b. If he ripostes with a mandritto or a fendente to your head, parry by getting with your sword into Guardia di Testa, and riposte with a mandritto to his head or leg (as you prefer).

    c. If he ripostes with a mandritto or a fendente to your leg, pass forward with your left foot, jam your false edge under the opponent's sword and give him a riverso to the leg, letting your right foot follow behind the left. Lastly, push a thrust to his face, jump backwards and recover in Coda Lunga e Alta.

7. If it was the opponent who executed the probing action with a thrust and a right-foot pass, to disrupt your guard and then attack you with a riverso to the head or forward leg, do the following. Defend against the thrust by hitting his sword-hand with a half mandritto ending in Cinghiara Porta di Ferro.

    a. As he delivers the riverso to your head, pass forward with your right foot and get with your sword into Guardia di Testa, thereby parrying. Ensure that your head is well guarded by your cape, and riposte with a mandritto to his head or leg (as you prefer).

    b. If his riverso was to your leg, pass forward with your right foot while executing a mezza volta with your sword-hand, your point down, thereby parrying the riverso. Then, immediately deliver a mandritto to his head. For your safety, pass back with your right foot and recover in Coda Lunga e Alta.

8. If the opponent tries to disrupt your guard with a mandritto or a fendente to the head, defend against any of these blows by passing back with your left foot and delivering a half mandritto into his sword-arm. Then, pass back with your right foot and recover in your original guard.

9. If he delivers a mandritto to your leg, pass back with your left foot while hitting his sword-hand with a mandritto; then, pass back with your right foot and recover in Coda Lunga e Alta.

10. If the opponent delivers a mandritto to your head, pass with your right foot to the opponent's right side and push a thrust that hits him in the face and in the sword-arm, while making yourself small under your thrust, ensuring your defense. Then, pass with your left foot towards his right side and strike him with a sideways riverso to his right leg; let your right foot follow behind the left. For your safety, push a thrust to his flank, retreat with a backward jump and recover in Coda Lunga e Alta.

---

[140] In Italian, *tentare il nemico*.

11. If the opponent attacks your head with a mandritto or riverso, parry by passing forward with your right foot and let your cape catch the blow; in the same tempo, push a thrust to his chest. Then, pass back with your right foot and protect yourself by going with your sword into Guardia di Faccia; pass back with your left foot and recover into Coda Lunga e Stretta (right foot forward).

Up to here, I have listed the actions from Coda Lunga e Alta (left foot forward) that are possible with the *spada da filo* and the cape. I will now move on to other equally useful actions from Coda Lunga e Stretta (right foot forward) in the same weapon combination. If you are in Coda Lunga e Stretta:

1. If the opponent attacks with a mandritto or fendente, parry by going into Guardia di Testa, immediately riposting with a mandritto to his leg. For your safety, pass back with your right foot while pushing a thrust into Guardia di Faccia, accompanied by the cape. Then, pass back with your left foot and turn your hand, thereby ending in Coda Lunga e Stretta with your right foot forward.

2. If the opponent attacks with a mandritto, you can also push a thrust to his face while making yourself small under your sword (thereby defending against his attack). Then, immediately pass with your left foot towards his right side and deliver a riverso to his leg, letting your right foot follow behind the left. For your safety, push a thrust to his face and retreat with a backward jump. Lastly, recover in Coda Lunga e Stretta.[141]

3. Against a mandritto to the head, you can also pass forward with your left foot and parry with the cape; then, push a thrust to his flank, retreat with a jump and recover in Coda Lunga e Stretta.

4. Against the same attack, you can also lift your cape into Guardia di Testa while delivering a half mandritto to his sword-arm, ending with your sword in Porta di Ferro Stretta. For your safety, pass back with your right foot and get with your sword into Guardia di Faccia, accompanied by the cape. Then, pass back with your left foot and recover into Coda Lunga e Stretta.

5. Against a mandritto to the leg, pass with your left foot towards the opponent's right side and jam your false edge under his attack; riposte with a riverso to the leg and let your right foot follow behind the left. For your safety, deliver a thrust to his face, retreat with a sprightly jump and recover in Coda Lunga e Stretta.

6. Against a mandritto to the leg, you can also pass back with your right foot and strike his sword-arm with a half mandritto; then, pass back with your left foot and recover in your original guard.

---

[141] The additional piece of footwork necessary to end up with the right foot forward is implied here and elsewhere in this chapter. This can be a forward or backward pass in conjunction with the thrust to the opponent's face, a switching of the feet executed while jumping backward or an additional backward pass executed after the jump.

7. If you are both in Coda Lunga e Stretta and you are the attacker, pass with your left foot towards the opponent's right side and push a thrust to his face. As he tries to parry, pass forward with your right foot, place your cape under his sword while (in the same tempo) withdrawing your sword-hand to then push a thrust to his flank. For your safety, pass back with your right foot while striking his sword-arm with a half mandritto ending in Cinghiara Porta di Ferro; then, pass back three or four times and recover in Coda Lunga e Stretta.

Chapter II: Fencing Two Against Two With the Sword and Cape

Be this an assalto or actual mortal combat, place yourself and your companion against your two adversaries—who will also be each-other's companions— in such a way that the four of you form a square. You will then silently agree with your friend to switch opponents by proceeding cross-wise, as I am about to describe.

Your companion will be to your right or to your left. If you are to the left, (according to the plan you have silently made) feint a thrust to the opponent immediately in front of you. Then, immediately interrupt the feinting action and pass strongly with the right foot towards your friend's opponent; use the cape to defend against your former opponent and strike your new one in the flank with the thrust originating from the feint.

Your companion must do the same as you—that is, not against his original opponent but against yours, with a similar crosswise path and a similar thrust to the flank.

In this manner, each of you will catch your friend's opponent by surprise, thereby obtaining the desired victory from a noble action.

Chapter III: Fencing with the *Spada da Filo* in the Right Hand and the Dagger in the Left

Set yourself with your left foot forward, your sword in Coda Lunga e Alta and your dagger in Porta di Ferro Stretta.

1. Gather forward with your right foot and pass forward with your left; this will force the opponent to either attack or retreat.

2. If he attacks you with a mandritto to your head, parry by getting with your dagger into Guardia di Testa; quickly pass with your right foot towards his left side while delivering a mandritto to the opponent's leg or a thrust to his flank. Let your left foot follow behind the right. For your safety, pass back three or four times and recover into your original guard.

3. If he attacks you with a thrust, parry it with the false edge of the dagger, while pushing a thrust of your own into his flank accompanied by an accrescimento of your left foot. For your safety, retreat with a backward jump and recover into your original guard.

4. If the opponent pushes a thrust to your face to attack you with a mandritto to the forward leg, parry the thrust with the dagger. As he releases the mandritto,

jam the false edge of your sword under his attack, pass with your right foot towards his left side and turn a mandritto to his head or leg. Let your left foot follow behind the right and place your dagger in Guardia di Testa. For your safety, pass back three or four times and recover in your original guard.

5. If the opponent pushes a thrust to attack your head or forward leg with a riverso, parry the thrust with your dagger. Parry the riverso (if it is to the leg) with your dagger also, point down, while in the same tempo thrusting your sword into his chest or hitting his sword-arm with a falso.

Chapter IV: Fencing with Sword and Rotella

Place yourself in a corner of the salle, with your sword in your hand and the rotella strapped to your arm, as elegantly as you can.

1. Pass with your left foot towards the opponent's right, then forward with your right, while doing falso and mandritto ending in Porta di Ferro in an oblique stance;[142] let your left foot follow behind the right.

2. Step with your right foot somewhat towards the opponent's left side, then pass with your left into a wide stance, in the same tempo doing falso and riverso; let your right foot follow behind your left and make sure your sword is in Coda Lunga e Alta.

3. Step with your left foot somewhat towards your right side, then pass forward with your right into a wide stance, while doing falso and mandritto ending with your sword in Porta di Ferro Larga; let your left foot follow behind the right.

4. Step with your right foot somewhat towards your left side, then forward with your left foot into a wide stance, doing falso and riverso; let your right foot follow behind the left and ensure your sword is in Coda Lunga e Alta. This will conclude the entry into the play.

And now, to light the flame of battle with your opponent (who at this point is close to you):

1. Push a thrust with your left foot forward.

2. Gather back with your left foot, extending your sword behind you, then pass forward with your right foot feinting a mandritto to his head. As he lifts his rotella in fear of your cut, you can do one of two things:

   a. Hit his leg with a riverso.

   b. Pass forward with your left foot and push a thrust to his flank; then retreat with a backward jump.

---

[142] Meaning that your feet are not in line with the opponent, but your right foot is to the right of the line.

3. If he is the one who attacks your leg with the riverso, pass back with your right foot and deliver a falso under your rotella, thereby remaining safe against his attack. Then, open your sword-arm[143] while returning into Coda Lunga.

4. Pass with your left foot towards his left, then forward with your right, delivering a falso and a mandritto to the opponent's sword-hand, ending with your sword in Porta di Ferro Larga; let your left foot follow behind the right.

5. Then, pass forward with your right foot towards the opponent's right, and forward with your left in a wide stance, in the same tempo delivering a falso and a riverso to his sword-arm; let your right foot follow behind your left.

6. Then, immediately gather back with your left foot, pass forward with your right and push a thrust to the opponent's face; then, feint a riverso and strike his forward leg with a mandritto, ending with your sword in Porta di Ferro Larga. Let your head be well defended by your rotella. Pass with your left foot towards his [...][144] side, while similarly defending with the rotella against his attack and delivering a riverso to his thigh. Let your right foot follow behind the left.

7. For your safety, push a thrust to his flank and retreat with a backward jump; then, pass forward with your right foot in a wide stance while pushing a thrust to his face and a riverso to his thigh.

8. Pass with your left foot towards the opponent's right side, jamming your false edge under your rotella, thereby defending against the mandritto with which the opponent may attack you; riposte with a riverso to his forward leg, then pass back with your left foot and get in Guardia di Faccia for your defense.

9. Pass with your left foot to the opponent's right side, delivering a fendente-like riverso; let your right foot follow behind the left.

10. Pass with your left foot towards the opponent's left side, then with the right foot, and push a thrust to his face followed by a mandritto to the leg ending in Porta di Ferro Larga; let your left foot follow behind the right.

11. Pass with your right foot towards the opponent's right side, then forward with your left foot, doing falso and riverso ending in a nice, extended Coda Lunga e Distesa. Then, gather forward with your right foot and pass forward with your left, lifting your rotella and striking the opponent in the face with a falso.

12. Pass back with your left foot and deliver a riverso to his face.

13. Pass back with your right foot and push a thrust under your rotella going into Guardia di Faccia; then, open your sword-arm and set yourself in Coda Lunga e Alta.

---

[143] This means that you will pull your sword-arm away from your rotella, thus "opening" your arms.

[144] Manciolino omits to say which side, but based on earlier plays, it is likely to the opponent's right side.

14. If the opponent attacks you, give him a falso to the sword-hand under your rotella, then immediately recover in guard.

15. Push a thrust with your left foot forward, pass back with your left foot, then with your right and get your sword into Coda Lunga e Distesa.

16. Immediately pass forward with your right foot and strike his head with a fendente ending in Porta di Ferro Larga; then pass back with your right foot.

17. As the opponent starts an attack, pass forward with your right foot and parry with a falso, riposting with a riverso to the head or forward leg.

18. For your safety, pass back with your right foot while pushing a thrust from under your rotella and ending with your sword in Guardia di Faccia, where you will parry his attack. Then, recover in Coda Lunga e Alta.

19. Push a thrust to his face with a right-foot pass; to do this, ensure that the opponent has his right foot forward.

20. Pass with your left foot towards his right side and strike a mandritto to the opponent's leg, ensuring that your head is well-defended by your rotella. Let your right foot follow behind the left.

21. Push a thrust to his face, retreating with a backward jump, and recover in your original guard.

22. If he attacks you with a mandritto or fendente to your head, pass with your right foot towards his right side while pushing a thrust to his face from under your rotella; let your thrust end in Guardia di Faccia, making yourself small under your sword, as it receives the opponent's blow.

23. Immediately pass with your left foot towards the opponent's right side, delivering a riverso to his forward leg; let your right foot follow behind the left.

24. For your safety, push a thrust to the opponent's face and retreat with a backward jump; then, recover in Coda Lunga e Alta.

25. If he attacks your leg with a mandritto, pass forward with your right foot and jam your false edge under your rotella, which will keep you safe from his cut; riposte with a riverso to his forward leg and (for your safety) pass back with your right foot while pushing a thrust from under your rotella and ending in Guardia di Faccia; then, pass back with your left foot and deliver a fendente-like mandritto ending in Porta di Ferro Stretta.

26. From there, push a thrust with a left-foot pass, then pass with your right foot toward the opponent's left and attack his head or leg with a mandritto ending in Porta di Ferro Stretta; let your left foot follow behind the right.

27. Pass back with your right foot and recover in Coda Lunga e Alta.

28. If he attacks your head with a mandritto, parry it with the rotella while doing a mezza volta with your body (without moving your feet).[145] Then, deliver a half mandritto to his sword-arm, ending in Cinghiara Porta di Ferro.

29. Immediately pass forward with your right foot and deliver an ascending falso to the opponent's sword-hand, then a riverso to his thigh with your sword ending in Coda Lunga e Stretta with your right foot forward. In this guard, you cannot deliver any blow that is not effective; I consider it to be the best for this type of play.

Once you finish the fight, if you want to elegantly retreat from the play:

1. Pass back with your right foot, doing falso and mandritto with your sword ending in Cinghiara Porta di Ferro

2. Pass back with your left foot, doing falso and riverso ending with your sword in Coda Lunga e Stretta

3. Pass back with your right foot, once again doing falso and mandritto ending in Cinghiara Porta di Ferro

4. Finish by passing back with your left foot, opening your sword-arm and recovering where you started in Coda Lunga e Alta

---

[145] The underlying principle of this action is similar to the *volta stabile* described by Fiore de' Liberi, author of the circa-1409 treatise *Fior di Battaglia*: it is essentially a turning of the body aided by pivoting on the balls of the stationary feet.

Book Six

I now wish to show how wrong those are who insist that good swordsmanship can never proceed from practice with blunted weapons, but only from training with sharp swords. First of all, is it with our heads that we learn and understand or with our feet? Since everyone will agree that it is with the former, let me ask something else: does our intellect grasp the actual objects before us or rather the ideas or likenesses of them?

I do not think anyone can be so silly as to claim that my students are learning the very art that is in me; rather, they are learning its effigy. Likewise, nobody can say that the pilgrim returning from Rome is actually carrying that physical city in his memory (how could its walls even fit inside his head?). Rather, the pilgrim will be carrying an image: and just by meditating on such image, he will be able to see Rome as if he were there—even as he walks the streets of Bologna.

Therefore, likenesses are so similar to what is real and what they represent that once one obtains them, he practically obtains the objects themselves. But such likenesses are of two kinds. Some, like the ones I have just described, only penetrate the intellect; these can only be seen by the person doing the thinking. The others, instead, transcend the intellect; these appear to everyone in the same manner—just as if someone else had my portrait. And the likenesses of the second type are by no means inferior to those of the first.

Indeed, how often have we seen real birds flock to feed on local grapes that, although appearing real, are skillfully painted on walls? What about fair Narcissus, who, beholding his own reflected image in a clear stream and not recognizing himself, fell in love? Also, when in our sacred cathedrals, do we not kneel before marble statues or painted images to adore our true God, although we know that what is before us is nothing but stone and color? And does the fact that God is not really before us take away from the goodness of worshipping at the images of His greatness?

Going back to matters closer to us, our art is not the only one in which likenesses (i.e., blunted swords and other comparatively safe weapons) take the place of the real objects they represent (sharp blades). Even waiters who serve food in rich banquets, if they want to excel at what they do, first practice their carving on roots and beets before applying their flying knives to meat.[146] Some even obtain wooden models of edible animals from lamb to game, made of interlocking components: and it is by practicing on these that they become perfect on real meat.

So, I wish those ignorant peasants would stop bleating about what they don't understand. It is far preferable to learn to strike with bated blades then with sharp ones; and it would not be fair to arm untrained students with sharp swords or with other weapons that can inflict injury for the purpose of training new students to defend themselves.

---

[146] Food carving was considered a veritable art in 16th-Century Italy. The preferred technique of the best carvers was to carve on the fork, over the plate—hence "flying knives." Carving was done as much for elegant food presentation as for practical purposes, and some important treatises appeared on the subject, such as the celebrated *Il Trinciante* by Vincenzo Cervio (Venice, 1581 and 1593).

Anyway, since I have already given sufficient instruction about fencing with shorter weapons, I will in this sixth book speak of the use of polearms. These weapons can be used with just as much grace and produce the same excellent results as the ones we have already seen. This book will contain two plays of rotella and partisan, one of two partisans, followed by the *spiedo*, the *ronca* and the spear. [147]

Play of Rotella and Partisan against the Same

Set yourself with the rotella strapped to your arm, and the partisan in your hand as if ready to cast it[148] to the opponent as he faces you with the same weapons and in the same posture.

If he were to attack you weapon-in-hand[149] to your left leg, pass with your right foot toward his left side and turn the iron of your partisan towards the ground; stretch your arm smartly towards the opponent's right, thereby defending yourself against his attack. Let your left leg follow behind the right. Then, give him a punta riversa to the chest, and retreat to safety by jumping backward. Perform a mezza volta with the partisan over your head, and recover into the same guard in which you began.

Alternatively, you could be the initiator of the attack I just described. If the opponent defends in the same manner, as soon as he passes forward with his right foot, jump backward and set yourself in the guard I described with your left foot forward.

You could also approach the opponent and feint a thrust to his face: as soon as he lifts his rotella in fear of your attack, change the direction of your attack to his body.[150] Then, retreat to safety by means of a rearward jump and recover in the guard I described, with your partisan held overhand.

But if you both decided to cast the partisans at one-another, and your opponent cast his first, perform an oblique pass with your right foot towards your right side: at the same time, extend your right arm outward, so that the iron of your partisan points down. Then, let your left foot follow behind the right. In this manner you will be safe from your opponent's cast.

If he were to cast again,[151] pull back with your left foot obliquely towards your left and extend your right arm towards your right, with the iron pointing to the ground; then, let your right foot follow the left. In this manner you will be safe against this second cast, and you will have returned in your guard.

---

[147] For more about the physical aspect of these weapons, please refer to the technical compendium on the Bolognese style.

[148] The partisan could be handled with either one or two hands. Also, it could either be used *manescamente*, or *a mano tenente* i.e., in the hands at all times, or cast. Manciolino says that the guard calls for an overhand (*sopramano*) position, i.e., the hand holding the weapon should be high.

[149] *Manescamente*, as opposed to attacking you by casting his weapon like a spear.

[150] *Cangiare la partigiana*; essentially, it is the act of disengaging (or performing a *cavazione*) around and presumably under the rotella.

[151] I assume that Manciolino intends that the opponent would have a second partisan to cast, as he does towards the end of the play of single partisan.

Another Play of the Same Weapons

This is another play of rotella and partisan. Although it is not as eye-catching as the one I just described, it is still very useful.

Start by gripping the partisan with your right hand near its base and with your left at the other end of the weapon, even though your rotella is still strapped to your left arm. The knuckles of both hands will be facing upwards. Let your partisan point somewhat to the opponent's right. Your left foot will be forward in a stance that is not too wide, and there you will be waiting for your opponent's attack.

If he attacks your leg, parry with your partisan by hitting into his blow to the outside, towards his left. Let your right hand be higher than usual so that you can better parry, and riposte immediately with a blow to his leg. Then, recover in the guard already described.

If he pushes a thrust to your face, lower your right hand so that the iron of your partisan points up, and in this manner you will parry his blow. Then, give him a thrust to the face or leg (as you wish), and recover in the guard I have described.

Play of Single Partisan

Start by gripping the partisan with your left hand forward, with the knuckles of both hands facing up. Set yourself with left foot forward in a wide stance, and with the partisan pointing obliquely to your left. If the opponent is in this same guard, or in any other for that matter, either one of you can start the action.

Let's suppose that the opponent is the first to strike, with a thrust aimed at your leg. Parry the blow by hitting into his incoming weapon towards the outside (that is, towards the opponent's left), with your right hand high and the iron of your partisan pointing down. Then, riposte with a thrust of your own to his flank or leg (as you prefer), retreating to safety with a rearward jump and recovering in your guard.

If the opponent attacks you with a thrust to the face or with a cut, push your right hand down so that the iron of your partisan ends up in front of the opponent's face. By doing this, you will defend from his attack. Then, riposte with a thrust to his flank.

If he casts his weapon at your leg, you can parry as I taught you in the play described earlier.[152] If he casts his weapon from above, seize your partisan with your left hand near the iron (with the knuckles of both hands facing up) and pass with your right foot towards his left side, parrying with the butt of your partisan. Let your left leg follow behind the right.

But if he has two partisans and casts the second one in a similar manner, perform an oblique pass with your left foot towards your left, doing at the same time a *volta* with your partisan so that your iron points down, and your left hand is lower than the right. Then, let your right leg follow behind your left, and recover yourself in the guard I described, the one where you were ready to cast.

---

[152] See the section at the end of the first play of partisan and rotella.

Plays of Spiedo against Spiedo

Set yourself with your left foot forward, holding your spiedo with your arms well extended away from your body. Keep your left hand low, and your right behind and quite high, so that the iron of your weapon points down and is ready to parry the opponent's attacks. And so that we can say it once and for all, when I talk about blows or attacks with polearms I refer to thrusts.[153]

If your opponent is in a similar guard and attacks you either high or low, parry by hitting into his blow towards your left; in this manner, you will be safe from his attack. Then, riposte with a good thrust to his flank, performing a simultaneous accrescimento with your left foot.

But if you feel stronger than your opponent, you can fork the wings of his spiedo with yours. Without letting go, force his weapon towards your left side, so as to then give him a thrust to the flank. If he turns his guard and comes with his right side, turn yours in the same way.[154]

This same action you can do with a *quadrello* or a *spontoon*, although the lack of wings prevents you from forking as you would do with the spiedo.

Plays of Ronca against Ronca

Set yourself against the opponent with your right foot forward, and grip your ronca with the left hand at the butt of the haft and the right hand forward. Turn toward the opponent in this form, and make sure that the horn of your ronca faces down.

With a smart right-foot accrescimento, push a thrust to the opponent's face—then push the iron downward and do a *straziamento*[155] to his arms, and push a second thrust to his chest. Retreat by means of a rearward jump, and set yourself a left-foot-forward guard with the iron high in the air as if ready to deliver a mandritto to the opponent's head, which is how you will go against him.

If he attacks you with a mandritto to the head, pass immediately with your right foot towards his left side, hitting his ronca with a mandritto of your own so as to cause his weapon to hit the ground. Then, push a thrust to his flank and retreat by means of a rearward jump. Recover in the same guard with the left foot forward and the ronca high as if ready to deliver a mandritto to the opponent's head.

---

[153] It is interesting how the terminology varies according to the weapon used. A thrust with a partisan is a *partigianata,* one with a spiedo a *spiedata* etc. Following Manciolino's advice, I have translated them all with "thrust," except for where the cut (occasionally used here in spite of Manciolino's own thrusting-only rule) is specifically called for.

[154] By "turning the guard," the author means switching to a right-hand-forward grip and a right-foot-forward stance. This may be done in various ways. One is to let your right hand slide forward along the haft until it touches the left, immediately bringing the left hand back where the right was—while simultaneously executing a forward or backward pass with a mezza volta of the body.

[155] A *straziamento* is a technique where the ripping power of the ronca's horn is used to lacerate the target while the weapon is pulled back. Literally, a laceration.

If the opponent attacks you again with a mandritto or a thrust to the leg, pass forward with your right foot, parrying his blows with an ascending falso and riposting with a thrust to his flank.

If he attacks you with a thrust to the face, pass as described, hit into his ronca with a mandritto and riposte with a thrust to his chest.

Play of Hand-held Spears, One against One

Begin by gripping your spear with your right hand and setting yourself with the right foot forward in a wide stance. Do this if your opponent is situated in the same guard and is the first to attack.

If, instead, he places his left foot forward while gripping his spear as if to cast it at you, respond by doing the exact same. However, do not remove the point of your spear from near the ground. As you push the first thrust,[156] hit the opponent's spear obliquely towards your left side, so that you can be free to strike him. Then, immediately pass with your right foot, then with the left, giving him a thrust to the flank.

If, instead, you wish to strike first, pass forward with your right foot, pushing a thrust designed to make him parry as you just did in the previous action. As he hits your spear, cast it at an oblique angle and let go of it; it will fall on his weapon towards his right side. Use that tempo to run against the butt of his spear, then unsheathe your sword or dagger (which you will be wearing at your side) and, reaching him thus unexpectedly, you will be able to strike him at will.

If he tries this cast at you, yank your spear backward with your right hand, letting it slide through your left hand up to the iron. In this manner, he will not be able to strike you with his sword or dagger. He too could perform this technique on you. But since few people really understand these actions, you will definitely have the advantage.

If you are in a left-foot-forward posture, you can pass forward with your right and strike your opponent with a thrust in the chest followed by a riverso riposte.[157]

If the opponent tries this on you, feint a four or five-step retreat, dragging your spear with you with your right hand. Then, hurl yourself towards your right as you run, grip your spear with both hands and go against him; as you will find him disordered, you will be able to push a thrust into his flank.

The counter to the action I have just described is this: take your spear in both hands as the opponent runs away from you, and as he starts to jump to the side hit him with your spear before he can comfortably grip his.

---

[156] This is likely a clerical error; it is the opponent who pushes the first thrust, as evidenced by the parry and by the wording of the next paragraph.

[157] This action (riverso riposte, *risposta riversa* in Italian) is not defined, and its nature is open to several different interpretations. The most likely is this: push the thrust with the right hand while passing with your left foot, and let the weapon slide through your open left hand (this is known as a *punta slanciata*). Then, recover your weapon by pulling it back with your left hand near the butt of the haft and the right hand forward; this places you in the position of delivering a thrust from the other side (that is, in the manner of a *punta riversa*).

This is another action you can use. Feint a thrust, which he will try to avert by passing back with his left foot. At that point, run four or five steps obliquely towards his left side: thus, finding him open, you will be able to push a thrust into his flank. This technique is very good when fighting one-on-one, and you can also perform it by running towards his right side. Here is the counter: as you see your opponent running, pass back with your right foot and grip your spear with your left hand, since you cannot be hit as you will be just as apt to strike as is he.

Also, you can deliver a thrust with your right foot forward, letting go of the spear with your left hand and pushing your right arm towards your left, so that your right flank ends right in front of the opponent's face and the point of your spear is to the left of him. Here, wait for his attack: as he strikes towards your flank, pass forward with your left foot, pushing your right hand far to your outside (that is, to your right)—thereby voiding his attack. Then, quickly grip your spear with your left hand, pass forward with your right foot and deliver a thrust to his chest.

The counter to what I have just described is as follows. As your opponent uncovers his body to defend himself, feint an attack. If he comes forward to do what you did in the previous paragraph, he will be completely open to your feint, and you may strike him at your will.

If you want to place your opponent out of your presence[158] to your advantage, this is what you do. If he has his left foot forward, switch your hands on your spear, so that your right hand is forward of the left, and pass forward with your right foot. Or if you started with your right hand forward, switch your hands to force your opponent out of presence; as you see him with his right foot forward, then you will know you have forced him out of presence. This hand-switch is something you do when both of you are inside each-other's presence to force the opponent outside it so that he cannot harm you.

If you are armed with a spear and are attacked by an opponent wielding a partisan, a ronca or a spiedo, grip your weapon at mid-haft. All you need is an arm's length of advantage or more between your weapon and his—and this will keep you safe. If you wanted to use the whole length of your spear against his shorter weapon, he could easily hit into it and run against you.

So let me end the book by repeating what I have already said. With all polearms, there is only a good way of striking, which is with the thrust.

And with this, I have finished my chapters or general rules on the gallant and warlike Art of Fencing.

Printed in Venice by Nicolo' d'Aristotile called Zoppino.[159] 1531.

---

[158] That means, so that his weapon is out of line while yours is aimed at him.

[159] This is the same Venetian printer who published some of Pietro Aretino's works, including the comedy *La Cortegiana*.